THE TWENTY-EIGHTH AMENDMENT TO THE CONSTITUTION: A SOLUTION TO THE CURRENT DETERIORATION OF THE UNITED STATES OF AMERICA

Written By:

Taylor Pope-Williams

Copyright © 2025 by Taylor Elliott Pope-Williams.

All rights reserved. No part of this publication may be reproduced, distributed, or transmitted in any form or by any means, including photocopying, recording, or other electronic or mechanical methods, without the prior written permission of the author, except in the case of brief quotations embodied in critical reviews and certain other non-commercial uses permitted by copyright law.

First, Second, Third, Fourth, Fifth, and Sixth Printing in 2017.

Seventh and Eighth Printing in 2020.

Ninth and Tenth Printing in 2021.

Eleventh and Twelfth Printing in 2025.

ISBN-13: 978-1545595435

ISBN-10: 1545595437

Table of Contents

The 28th Amendment to the Constitution	5
Section One	13
Section Two	14
Section Three	15
Section Four	16
Section Five	18
Section Six	19
Section Seven	20
Section Eight	25
Section Nine	26
Section Ten	27
Section Eleven	28
Section Twelve	37
Section Thirteen	38
Section Fourteen	39
Section Fifteen	40
Section Sixteen	41
Section Seventeen	42
Section Eighteen	47
Section Nineteen	49
Section Twenty	50
Section Twenty-One	51
Section Twenty-Two	53
Section Twenty-Three	54
Section Twenty-Four	55
Section Twenty-Five	62
Section Twenty-Six	65
Section Twenty-Seven	66
Section Twenty-Eight	67
Section Twenty-Nine	68

Section Thirty	69
Section Thirty-One	70
Section Thirty-Two	71
Section Thirty-Three	74
Section Thirty-Four	76
Section Thirty-Five	77
Section Thirty-Six	78
Section Thirty-Seven	81
Section Thirty-Eight	82
Section Thirty-Nine	83
Section Forty	84
Section Forty-One	85
Section Forty-Two	86
Section Forty-Three	87
Section Forty-Four	89
Section Forty-Five	90
Free-Enterprise vs. Capitalism	92
Four Hour Workday	95
Federal Reserve Act: Transition Period	96
Bible Verses on Interest/Usury	97
Prescriptive Bible Verses on Polygyny/Polygamy	101
Why this Amendment and the Future Fight	103
Conclusion	105
Appendix: "The Economy of the Promise Land" by Anthony Migchels	110
A Review by Metin Ozsavran	113
Bibliography	114

The 28th Amendment to the Constitution:

Section One: Article One, Section Eight, Line One, which states "to borrow money on the credit of the United States," shall be nullified. In addition, the Public Debt of the United States shall be nullified.

Section Two: All debts incurred to the United States by foreign nations prior to the enactment of this amendment shall be nullified. In addition, all debts incurred to the United States after the enactment of this amendment shall be nullified every ten years on the fourth day of July, 12:00am.

Section Three: Deposits in financial institutions operating in the United States or any place subject to its jurisdiction, shall not be classified as debt.

Section Four: All debts incurred in the United States or any place subject to its jurisdiction prior to the enactment of this amendment shall be nullified. In addition, all debts incurred in the United States or any place subject to its jurisdiction after the enactment of this amendment shall be nullified every ten years on the fourth day of July, 12:00am.

Section Five: All debts incurred to persons residing in; corporations created and operating in; and financial institutions created and operating in the United States or any place subject to its jurisdiction by persons, corporations, and financial institutions in foreign nations prior to the enactment of this amendment, shall be nullified. In addition, all debts incurred to persons residing in; corporations created and operating in; and financial institutions created and operating in the United States or any place subject to its jurisdiction by persons, corporations, and financial institutions in foreign nations after the enactment of this amendment, shall be nullified every ten years on the fourth day of July, 12:00am.

Section Six: Article One, Section Eight, Line Five shall state "to create money, regulate the value thereof, and of foreign money, and fix the standards of weights and measures."

Section Seven: Representative Money and Commodity Money shall not be legal tender in or the lawful money of the United States.

Section Eight: Congress shall issue Notes and Coins. In addition, these Notes and Coins shall be legal tender and, alone, be the lawful money of the United States.

Section Nine: The right to obtain or possess tangible forms of the money of the United States; to use tangible forms of the money of the United States to pay debts; or to use tangible forms of the money of the United States to purchase goods or services, shall not be denied or abridged.

Section Ten: The right to obtain or possess intangible money other than the intangible money of the United States; to use intangible money other than the intangible money of the United States to pay debts; and to use intangible money other than the intangible money of the United States to purchase goods or services, shall not be denied or abridged.

Section Eleven: Charging Interest or derivatives of the aforementioned on money in the United States or any place subject to its jurisdiction, shall be prohibited. In addition, charging Fees or derivatives of the aforementioned on credit, loans, and debts in the United States or any place subject to its jurisdiction, shall be prohibited.

Section Twelve: The United States shall not charge Interest or Fees or derivatives of the aforementioned on credit or loans to, as well as on debts of persons, corporations, or governments of foreign nations. In addition, no person residing; corporation created and operating; or financial institution created and operating in the United States or any place subject to its jurisdiction, shall charge Interest or Fees or derivatives of the aforementioned on credit or loans to, as well as on debts of persons, corporations, or financial institutions in foreign nations.

Section Thirteen: No person, corporation, or financial institution in the United States or any place subject to its jurisdiction, shall be required by law to provide credit or a loan without obtaining collateral from the potential recipient of the aforementioned credit or loan.

Section Fourteen: No person, corporation, or financial institution in the United States or any place subject to its jurisdiction, shall be required by law to return collateral to the recipient of credit or a loan, if the aforementioned recipient has not reimbursed the full amount of the money that was borrowed from the aforementioned person, corporation, or financial institution. In addition, this section shall not be so construed as to affect any recipient of credit or a loan before it becomes valid as part of the Constitution.

Section Fifteen: Congress shall establish a bank. This bank shall provide deposit accounts to the residents of, corporations operating in, and residents of foreign nations aligned with the United States. In addition, this bank shall provide credit; loans; the ability to send or receive money; the ability to purchase or sell goods or services; and the ability to purchase or sell stocks of corporations to the residents of, corporations operating in, and residents of foreign nations aligned with the United States.

Section Sixteen: The right to put money in or withdraw money from; obtain credit or loans from; pay debts through; send or receive money through; purchase or sell goods or services through; or purchase or sell stocks of corporations through financial institutions other than the bank created by Congress, shall not be denied or abridged.

Section Seventeen: With exception to income, nothing shall be taxed in the United States or any place subject to its jurisdiction. This tax shall be collected once a year. For Congress, this tax shall be collected on the fifteenth day of April. For the States and Territories of the United States, this tax shall be collected on the thirtieth day of April. For the Counties and Municipalities in the United States and its Territories, this tax shall be collected on the fifteenth day of May.

Section Eighteen: Congress, the States, the Territories of the United States, and the Counties and Municipalities within the United States and its Territories shall tax no more than ten percent of incomes. Congress shall only tax persons that reside in the United States and its Territories. States, Territories, Counties, and Municipalities shall only tax persons that have declared the aforementioned areas as their primary residence.

Section Nineteen: No person that earns an income that is below the amount of income declared to be the threshold of poverty by Congress, shall be taxed by Congress. No person that earns an income that is below the amount of income declared to be the threshold of poverty by Congress, if they reside in the District that constitutes the seat of Government of the United States, shall be taxed by the aforementioned District. No person that earns an income below the amount of income declared to be the threshold of poverty by the State or Territory of the United States that they reside in, shall be taxed by the aforementioned State or Territory of the United States. And no person that earns an income below the amount of income declared to be the threshold of poverty by the State or Territory of the United States that they reside in, shall be taxed by the County and or Municipality that they reside in.

Section Twenty: No person that is below the age of twenty-one years old, shall be taxed.

Section Twenty-One: No person serving in the Armed Forces of the United States shall be taxed. No person that is honorably discharged from the Armed Forces of the United States due to receiving a severe permanent injury while serving in the Armed Forces of the United States, shall be taxed for the remainder of their life. No person that has been honorably discharged after serving twenty-five years or more in the Armed Forces of the United States shall be taxed for the remainder of their life. And none of the aforementioned persons shall be deprived of their status of honorable discharge as punishment for a crime in the United States or any place subject to its jurisdiction, unless the aforementioned crime be treason against the United States, whereof they have been duly convicted.

Section Twenty-Two: No corporation created or operating in the United States or its Territories, shall be taxed.

Section Twenty-Three: No person below the age of eighteen years old, shall be permitted to marry or enter a cohabitation agreement in the United States or any place subject to its jurisdiction. In addition, no person shall be punished in the United States or any place subject to its jurisdiction for the act of refusing to marry, enter a cohabitation agreement, practice procreation, or adopt children.

Section Twenty-Four: Marriage or a cohabitation agreement between persons of the same sex or gender; persons of different races, ethnicities, skin colors, national origins, creeds, or socioeconomic statuses; a non-disabled person and disabled person, if the aforementioned disabled person is capable; a non-cyborg and cyborg; a human and robot; two persons exclusively; one person of the male sex or gender and multiple persons of the female sex or gender; one person of the female sex or gender and multiple persons of the male sex or gender; a group of more than two persons of one sex or gender; and a group of more than two persons that is a mixture of sexes or genders, shall not be prohibited in the United States or any place subject to its jurisdiction.

Section Twenty-Five: Palimony, Alimony, Child Support, or derivatives of the aforementioned, shall be prohibited in the United States or any place subject to its jurisdiction.

Section Twenty-Six: The right of a person to divorce or terminate a cohabitation agreement in the United States or any place subject to its jurisdiction, shall not be denied or abridged. In addition, a person shall not be required to submit evidence of wrongdoing to a court of law in order to obtain a divorce or terminate a cohabitation agreement in the United States or any place subject to its jurisdiction.

Section Twenty-Seven: Any property obtained by a person, without receiving aid from their fiance or partner or obtaining it through committing an act of fraud or misappropriation towards their fiance or partner, prior to a marriage with the aforementioned fiance or cohabitation agreement with the aforementioned partner, irregardless if ownership of the aforementioned property is subsequently gifted to or jointly owned with their spouse or partner during the aforementioned marriage or cohabitation agreement, shall, upon divorce or termination of the aforementioned cohabitation agreement, be retained by the aforementioned person. In addition, any property obtained by a person without receiving aid from their spouse or partner during a marriage or cohabitation agreement, unless obtained through committing an act of fraud or misappropriation towards the aforementioned spouse or partner, upon divorce or termination of the aforementioned cohabitation agreement, irregardless if ownership of the aforementioned property is subsequently gifted to or jointly owned with their spouse or partner, shall be retained by the aforementioned person.

Section Twenty-Eight: The right to obtain an abortion in the United States or any place subject to its jurisdiction, shall not be denied or abridged.

Section Twenty-Nine: The right to obtain contraceptives in the United States or any place subject to its jurisdiction, shall not be denied or abridged.

Section Thirty: No Filial Responsibility or derivatives of the aforementioned, shall exist in the United States or any place subject to its jurisdiction.

Section Thirty-One: The right of a terminally ill person, who is of sound mind and not below the age of eighteen years old, to choose to end their own life with the aid of a physician in the United States or any place subject to its jurisdiction, shall not be prohibited.

Section Thirty-Two: No corporation shall be anonymously created or anonymously operated in the United States or any place subject to its jurisdiction. In addition, no corporation shall be permitted to create or operate a subsidiary corporation in the United States or any place subject to its jurisdiction, that does not declare its purpose within or practice its purpose as expressed within its articles of incorporation or charter.

Section Thirty-Three: No corporation created and operating in the United States or any place subject to its jurisdiction, shall be required by law to achieve a profitable return on investment capital to stockholders.

Section Thirty-Four: No Minimum Wage or derivatives of the aforementioned, shall exist in the United States or any place subject to its jurisdiction. In addition, the wages or earnings of a person working in the United States or any place subject to its jurisdiction shall consist of nothing other than the money of the United States.

Section Thirty-Five: No business in the United States or any place subject to its jurisdiction, shall be required by law to suspend operations during an epidemic or pandemic.

Section Thirty-Six: No copyright, patent, or derivatives of the aforementioned, shall exist in the United States or any place subject to its jurisdiction. In addition, no copyright, patent, or derivative of the aforementioned filed in a foreign nation, shall be enforced by a court of law in the United States or any place subject to its jurisdiction.

Section Thirty-Seven: No person appointed as Justice to the Supreme Court of the United States, shall serve more than twenty-five years. In addition, this section shall not be so construed as to affect the appointment of any Justice before it becomes valid as part of the Constitution.

Section Thirty-Eight: No solitary confinement of prisoners, shall be practiced in the United States or any place subject to its jurisdiction.

Section Thirty-Nine: Slavery or involuntary servitude as punishment for a crime, shall be prohibited in the United States or any place subject to its jurisdiction.

Section Forty: The right of citizens of the United States to vote shall not be denied or abridged by the United States, by any State, or by any Territory on account of conviction or imprisonment for a crime, unless the aforementioned crime is treason against the United States.

Section Forty-One: The right to borrow, loan, rent, own, sell, purchase, gift, bequeath, or inherit property in or outside of; to put money in, withdraw money from, send money to or from a financial institution in or outside of; to obtain credit or a loan in or outside of; to purchase goods or services in or outside of; to sell goods or services in or outside of; to work in or outside of; to obtain an education in or outside of; to serve in the Armed Forces of; to serve as a witness in a trial in a court of law in or outside of; to serve as juror in a court of law in or outside of; to a file a case in a court of law in or outside of; to invoke Habeas Corpus in; to create, enter, amend, leave, or terminate a contract in or outside of; to vote in or outside of; to hold public office in or outside of; to travel in, to, or from, the United States or any place subject to its jurisdiction, shall not be denied or abridged on the account of sex; gender; sexual orientation; race; ethnicity; skin color; creed; socioeconomic status; creed; marital status; childlessness or number of children possessed; disability, unless not capable; or national origin, unless it pertains to holding the office of President of the United States.

Section Forty-Two: The manufacture, sale, purchase, possession, or transportation of cannabis, psilocybin mushrooms, or byproducts of the aforementioned within, the importation thereof into, or the exportation thereof from the United States or any place subject to its jurisdiction, shall not be prohibited.

Section Forty-Three: Sex work and prostitution shall not be prohibited in the United States or any place subject to its jurisdiction. In addition, no person below the age of eighteen years old, shall be permitted to practice sex work or prostitution in the United States or any place subject to its jurisdiction.

Section Forty-Four: Conscription into the Armed Forces of the United States, including during times of rebellion, insurrection, or invasion, shall be prohibited.

Section Forty-Five: Congress shall have the power to enforce this article by appropriate legislation.

Section One:

"Article One, Section Eight, Line One, which states "to borrow money on the credit of the United States," shall be nullified. In addition, the Public Debt of the United States shall be nullified."

In regard to the first sentence of Section One of this amendment, there are two reasons for its existence: 1.) It's to eliminate a defect within the Constitution of the United States. 2.) It's to force Congress to enact Section Six of this amendment, which is the creation and regulation of the money supply of the United States.

In regard to the second sentence of Section One of this amendment, the reason for its existence is to end the postponement of the inevitable, which is the United States defaulting on its debt.

Results of Enactment

1. It will make the Federal Reserve System irrelevant.[1]
2. It will prevent the United States from becoming indebted in the future.[2]

---

[1] One of the responsibilities of the Federal Reserve System is to sell the debt (bonds) of the United States to public and private entities.

[2] In *Secrets of the Federal Reserve,* page 66, Eustace Mullins provides a quotation from Henry Claws, which stated that the destruction of the Second Bank of the United States brought forth financial prosperity to America. This resulted in the Federal Government paying off the National Debt and storing $50 million in the United States Treasury.

According to https://www.officialdata.org/us/inflation: $50,000,000 (1837) would translate into an estimated $1,675,000,000 (2025).

Section Two:

"All debts incurred to the United States by foreign nations prior to the enactment of this amendment shall be nullified. In addition, all debts incurred to the United States after the enactment of this amendment shall be nullified every ten years on the fourth day of July, 12:00am."

There are two reasons for the existence of Section Two of this amendment: 1.) To placate foreign nations after the United States defaults on its debt. 2.) To prevent the United States from oppressing foreign nations in the future with debt.

Section Three:

"Deposits[3] in financial institutions operating in the United States or any place subject to its jurisdiction, shall not be classified as debt."

The reason for the existence of Section Three of this amendment is to prevent the destitution of the American People, which, otherwise, would have occurred under Section Four of this amendment.

---

[3] The author originally wanted to include Judgment Debts in this section, but, due to realizing that it can be used as a loophole for Section Four of this amendment, refrained from doing so. As a result, the United States will have to find an alternative to financial compensation for Punitive and Compensatory Damages.

There are three alternatives that the author thinks are considerable: corporal punishment, retribution, or imprisonment. The first two punishments, which the author learned through his study of theonomy, are not possible. Corporal punishment (e.g. flogging) violates the Eight Amendment of the United States Constitution. Retribution, which is encapsulated in the phrase "eye for an eye, tooth for a tooth" and elaborated upon in parts of the Bible (e.g. Exodus 21:28-31 and Exodus 22:1-4) is not always practical (e.g. compensating the owner of a damaged, misplaced, stolen, or destroyed one-of-a-kind object).

Section Four:

"All debts incurred in the United States or any place subject to its jurisdiction prior to the enactment of this amendment shall be nullified. In addition, all debts incurred in the United States or any place subject to its jurisdiction after the enactment of this amendment shall be nullified every ten years[4] on the fourth day of July, 12:00am."

"At the end of every seven years,[5] you shall cancel debts. This is the way it shall be done: every creditor shall release that which he has lent to his neighbor. He shall not require payment from his neighbor and his brother, because Yahweh's release has been proclaimed. Of a foreigner you may require it; but whatever of yours is with your brother, your hand shall release. However there will be no poor with you (for Yahweh will surely bless you in the land which Yahweh your God gives you for an inheritance to possess) if only you diligently listen to Yahweh your God's voice, to observe to do all this commandment which I command you today. For Yahweh your God will bless you, as he promised you. You will lend to many nations, but you will not borrow. You will rule over many nations, but they will not rule over you. If a poor man, one of your brothers, is with you within any of your gates in your land which Yahweh your God gives you, you shall not harden your heart, nor shut your hand from your poor brother; but shall surely open your hand to him, and shall surely lend him sufficient for his need, which he lacks. Beware that there not be a wicked thought in your heart, saying, 'The seventh year, the year of release, is at hand,' and your eye be evil against your poor brother and you give him nothing; and he cry to Yahweh against you, and it be sin to you. You shall surely give, and your heart shall not be grieved when you give to him, because it is for this thing Yahweh your God will bless you in all your work and in all that you put your hand to. For the poor will never cease out of the land. Therefore I command you to surely open your hand to your brother, to your needy, and to your poor, in your land."

– Deuteronomy 15: 1-11 (World English Bible)

---

4   The author chose ten years instead of seven (or three) because he thought it would create a less tumultuous economy.
5   Fun Fact: The Code of Hammurabi, which existed before the creation of the Old Testament and served as a template for the Mosaic Laws, demanded that nullification of debts every three years.

Results of Enactment

1. **Reduces the Financial Burden of the Federal, State, and Territorial Governments.**
   I. It will eliminate bail-outs.
   II. It will reduce the number of recipients of government programs.
   - For example, due to possessing money previously directed towards the payment of debts, more people will be able to afford the adoption of children. This would lead to a reduction in the number of children that the government will need to take care of.

2. **Reduces the Cost of Goods and Services.**
   I. It will eliminate loan costs, which are passed onto bystanders (e.g. tenants, and customers) via prices.
   II. Businesses, utilizing money previously directed towards the payment of debts, will be able to use that money to speed up the production process or expand operations, which will reduce the price of goods and services.

3. **Reduces Abortions and use of Contraceptives.**

   Men and women, utilizing money previously directed towards the payment of debts, will be able to afford either having children in general or expanding the number of children they have.

4. **Revitalizes the Economy.**
   I. People, no longer fearing indebtedness, will be incentivize to pursue college and vocational training.[6] This will create more entrepreneurs and employees.
   II. Businesses, utilizing money previously directed towards the payment of debts, will be able to increase the wages of their employees and or expand their operations.
   III. Increase in wages and decrease in unemployment will lead to more consumer spending, which, in turn, will lead to businesses increasing the wages of their employees and or expanding operations (which decreases unemployment).

---

6   Another option is the government making college and vocational schooling completely free.

Section Five:

"All debts incurred to persons residing in; corporations created and operating in; and financial institutions created and operating in the United States or any place subject to its jurisdiction by persons, corporations, and financial institutions in foreign nations prior to the enactment of this amendment, shall be nullified. In addition, all debts incurred to persons residing in; corporations created and operating in; and financial institutions created and operating in the United States or any place subject to its jurisdiction by persons, corporations, and financial institutions in foreign nations after the enactment of this amendment, shall be nullified every ten years on the fourth day of July, 12:00am."

There are two reasons for the existence of Section Five of this amendment: 1.) To placate foreign citizens and corporations after the debt nullification enacted in Section Four of this amendment. 2.) To prevent American citizens and corporations from oppressing foreign citizens and corporations in the future with debt.

Section Six:

"Article One, Section Eight, Line Five shall state "to create money, regulate the value thereof, and of foreign money, and fix the standards of weights and measures."

There are two reasons for the existence of Section Six of this amendment: 1.) It's to make it obvious to the general public that Congress is designated with the task of creating and regulating the money supply of the United States. 2.) It eliminates a defect within the Constitution of the United States, which is when Congress creates money, it is both not limited to creating coinage and able to produce paper notes.[7]

Why should Congress "create" money?

In *History of Money and Usury in America,* page 9, Daniel Krynicki writes the following:

"Consider the following: Money must have a beginning; that is, it must be created before it can circulate. When it is created as direct payment for any services performed, it has value in the service performed, or in the finished product that was purchased. If the government paid for the building of a bridge over a waterway out of created fiat money, the bridge itself would indeed be an equity that is testament to the value of the money. In this way money would actually be created and then given in return for the labor and materials needed to pay for something. Now the money that paid for the bridge remains in circulation unless or until it is taxed out of existence. So while this money remains in circulation, it still has value. If money is borrowed at interest from private money creators to pay for the bridge, the cost of the bridge may double, triple or possibly go even higher depending upon both the term of the loan and the interest rate. Under our present system, when the principal and interest of the bridge loan is paid back to a private lender, the principal vanishes from the currency stream. At that point the money disappears; but real wealth has been realized in the bridge; and the moneylender has made a neat profit for simply doing some accounting."[8]

---

[7] While the Legal Tender Cases of 1871 and the case of "Julliar v. Greenman" declare paper notes created by Congress to be Constitutional, it must be remembered that they are only court verdicts. In other words, they can be overturned and, due to the fact that it is verdicts of the Supreme Court and not a law passed by Congress, they can be overturned quickly.

[8] Watson Institute of International and Public Affairs, Brown University, provides an example of this: "The current wars have been paid for almost entirely by borrowing. This borrowing has raised the US budget deficit, increased the national

Section Seven:

"Representative Money and Commodity Money shall not be legal tender in or the lawful money of the United States."

What does "legal tender" and "lawful money" mean?

The author wrote the words "legal tender" and "lawful money" with the definitions provided by Investopedia[9] in mind. According to this website, Legal Tender is money recognized by the Federal Government to settle debts (e.g. Paper Currency and Checks), while Lawful Money is currency issued by the Federal Government (e.g. Gold and Silver Coins; Treasury Notes; and Treasury Bonds).

The Reason for this Section

The reason for the existence of Section Seven of this amendment is to prevent the money supply of the United States from being controlled by the International Bankers through precious metals (gold and silver).

Why not Gold and Silver?

In *Digest of the Divine Law,* pages 83 to 85, Howard B. Rand writes the following about the Gold Standard:

"Under virgin conditions and in a primitive state men practised barter and exchanged their labor and goods for the labor and goods of others. As a nation increased its wealth, and commercial activities multiplied, a medium of exchange became necessary whereby purchasing power might be stored for future use. The volume of that medium of exchange would control the price of goods and because this is so there is only one equitable basis against which that medium should be issued and it is not gold!

---

debt, and had other macroeconomic effects, such as raising consumer interest rates. Unless the US immediately repays the money borrowed for war, there will also be future interest payments. We estimate that interest payments could total over $7.9 trillion by 2053." (http://watson.brown.edu/costsofwar/costs/economic)

9   Investopedia article *Law Money: Meaning, Overview, and History* (https://www.investopedia.com/terms/l/lawfulmoney.asp).

Under our system gold, an inflexible standard, has been selected, and because it has been accepted as the standard of commercial operation in order, therefore, to always keep a true balance, increase in labor and goods decreases prices while the reverse is true when there is a decrease in labor and goods' prices increase. This trends towards poverty and distress for the many, while wealth has a tendency to gravitate into the hands of the few.

"In barter, an increase of labor results in an increase of goods which could be exchanged for the increased wealth of others. Thus the industrious through labor could increase their wealth. Under a system which has gold for its standard of value, the increase of goods (the result of increased labor) may increase the poverty of the laborer through a sharp decline in values as the result of the inability of the medium of exchange to expand in the same ratio as the increase in goods. The vicious circle is completed by thus making the possession of gold more valuable than the possession of property.

"In order today to control prices, and keep a more equitable balance between goods and prices, instead of discarding the present (1943) arbitrary standard of value and adopting the Divine method, men decree the destruction of goods and the curtailment of production. Thus real wealth, the things men can use and eat, are destroyed to prevent inflation, the result of the inability of the present medium of exchange to expand with the increase in production. Inflation would never occur under the God-given system, for there the medium of exchange is wholly adequate to handle the abundance that God has provided through allowing men to discover the means for increasing the production of the farm and the factory.

"Today, with the increase in wealth there is a corresponding increase in poverty with periodic depressions, and despite the fact that we are in a land capable of yielding in abundance we experience untold wealth on one hand and dire poverty and distress on the other.

"In our national desire for continued monetary prosperity, and in order to save a system of exchange not based upon real wealth, true wealth is destroyed that the gold standard may continue to function that the few may be prosperous. What a travesty of intelligence to hold, when God abundantly increases our goods, that prosperity can be had only by destruction or curtailment of that increase.

"Increased possessions should spell PROSPERITY with capital letters and it should never mean adversity. The very fact that it does not do so is a condemnation of the system that fails to give liberally to the laborer his or her share in that increase.

"With food enough for all, thousands are on the verge of starvation; with enough to clothe all, many are underclad; with an abundance of fuel, thousands suffer with the cold. The reason for this is due to the failure of the system of exchange that has become wealth. That system, valueless in itself, yet, because of the fact that it can earn upon itself, has taken the place of true wealth which must be destroyed to sustain the present system of values which is wholly inadequate to meet the needs of life in such abundance as God is now willing to give unto men. The inflexibility of the interest-bearing gold standard prevents thousands from converting their labor into the necessities of life."

In *History of Money and Usury in America,* pages 8 to 9, Daniel Krynicki writes the following about the Gold Advocates:

"Fiat money is money that derives its value from government regulation or law (From Wikipedia). **[4]** The Colonial American governments also emitted fiat paper money known as 'Bills of Credit'. Some of these were legal tender. During the Civil War, the US government issued two types of fiat paper currency notes to pay Union troops and other expenditures needed to prosecute the war **[7].** The gold advocates referred to them as 'Greenbacks' and claim that nothing backed them. We will show herein that their disdain for fiat money is not justified. Any legal tender created by edict (or fiat if you will) is always backed by collateral, that is, by the people with their assets and labor. Furthermore, when a government emits this fiat money, as payment directly in return for labor and infrastructure that is needed as well as funding the costs of government, that labor, infrastructure and government services actually give the created money real value. Something useful has been received in return for the money that was created. We can call this money legal tender upon which no interest has to be paid and it remains in circulation as 'purchasing power' by whomever it was paid to. This money will also be legal tender even if it only appears on our radar in an account balance as cyberspace digits. It is the sort that Thomas Edison identified in his famous Mussel Shoals editorial letter from the 1920's **[8]**. With this type of money a government creates legal tender notes, fiat money, Greenbacks or 'bills of credit', whatever the snide usurers decide to call them, to pay directly for infrastructure projects without borrowing and without paying interest to anyone and without paying back principal to anyone. This money is not borrowed; it is issued.

"Article 1 Section 8 Line 5 of the Constitution explicitly authorizes Congress to do this. But instead of creating money in this way, Congress and an idiot President passed the Federal Reserve Act on December 23, 1913 giving this authority to create our money over to a cartel of international bankers. Elected officials in our national government therefore do not have either the intelligence or the wit to issue the money our nation needs to conduct its business. And instead of lending, usury free credit to its own citizens, of this money and credit that it has the authority to create, it borrows from these international criminal cartels almost everything that enters our currency stream.

"Presently, loaning of credit at interest by private banks depends only on the ability of the borrower to pay back the loan and the collateral being purchased by the borrower. These are two necessary components in the terms of any loan; and the loan process involves a contract spelling out terms with signatures. We can call this bank credit 'money' because it actually acts as money in our present system. [9] Earlier on in our history it was known as 'book credit' as Professor Davis Rich Dewey called it during the early twentieth century. Credit cards fall under this definition. All in all, it comprises about 97% of our circulating money supply because the exchange of Treasury Bonds for Federal Reserve notes is merely an elaborate variation of book credit. Credit is suitable for use as money because 90% of the business world accepts it as payment for their products or services. Technically, though, it does not fall under the definition of legal tender. There is no gold or any other commodity to purportedly back it, so it greatly resembles fiat money. But when push comes to shove all money allowed into the currency stream legally is fiat money. The gold advocates miss the whole point. Even their purportedly 'gold backed money' is also fiat. That is, it is nothing but paper or linen with ink, or cyberspace ledger entries upon which they expect to collect usury."

Fiat Money

In the article *Paper that is as good as Gold,*[10] Robert Bruce Record states the following:
1. Money is merely a tool to ease the exchange of goods and services, it is not a commodity.
2. Money is the measurement of wealth, not wealth itself.
3. The true wealth of the American People are the goods and services they create.
4. Irregardless if the money of the United States is made from paper or minerals, said money is only valuable if the Federal Government declares it to be a medium-of-exchange. As a result, paper is not less valuable than gold or silver.

Results of Enactment

1. It would prevent the destruction of the United States through a Gold Standard.[11]

---
10 https://hopeofthenation.com/paper-that-is-as-good-as-gold.html#/
11 In 1932, seven years after re-introducing the Gold Standard to the United Kingdom, Winston Churchill admitted to the

2. It would eliminate the ability of State Governments to declare gold and silver coins to be legal tender (Article 1, Section 10, Clause 1).

House of Commons that such an action was a mistake. (https://recoveringaustrians.wordpress.com/2012/01/25/winston-churchill-testifying-on-the-gold-standard-he-had-introduced-himself/).

Section Eight:

"Congress shall issue Notes and Coins. In addition, these Notes and Coins shall be legal tender and, alone, be the lawful money of the United States."

In regard to the first sentence of Section Eight of this amendment, the reason for its existence is to make the Federal Government resume making United States Notes. Meanwhile, the reason for the second sentence of Section Eight of this amendment is to eliminate Federal Reserve Notes.

Results of Enactment

It will create an interest-free and debt-free currency for the United States, while simultaneously removing interest-laden and debt-laden currency from circulation.[12]

---

[12] Federal Reserve Notes are representations of the debt (bonds) of the United States that are circulating among the purchasers of said debt (bonds).

Section Nine:

"The right to obtain or possess tangible forms of the money of the United States; to use tangible forms of the money of the United States to pay debts; or to use tangible forms of the money of the United States to purchase goods or services, shall not be denied or abridged."

The reason for the existence of Section Nine of this amendment is to prevent the creation of a cashless society.

Section Ten:

"The right to obtain or possess intangible money other than the intangible money of the United States; to use intangible money other than the intangible money of the United States to pay debts; and to use intangible money other than the intangible money of the United States to purchase goods or services, shall not be denied or abridged."

The reason for the existence of Section Ten of this amendment is to prevent private cryptocurrencies from being eliminated by the Federal Government; especially if said Federal Government creates its own cryptocurrency.

Section Eleven:

"Charging Interest or derivatives of the aforementioned on money in the United States or any place subject to its jurisdiction, shall be prohibited. In addition, charging Fees or derivatives of the aforementioned on credit, loans, and debts[13] in the United States or any place subject to its jurisdiction, shall be prohibited."

"But I tell you who hear: love your enemies, do good to those who hate you, bless those who curse you, and pray for those who mistreat you. To him who strikes you on the cheek, offer also the other; and from him who takes away your cloak, don't withhold your coat also. Give to everyone who asks you, and don't ask him who takes away your goods to give them back again. As you would like people to do to you, do exactly so to them. If you love those who love you, what credit is that to you? For even sinners love those who love them. If you do good to those who do good to you, what credit is that to you? For even sinners do the same. If you lend to those from whom you hope to receive, what credit is that to you? Even sinners lend to sinners, to receive back as much. But love your enemies, and do good, and ***lend, expecting nothing back***; and your reward will be great, and you will be children of the Most High; for he is kind toward the unthankful and evil. Therefore be merciful, even as your Father is also merciful. Don't judge, and you won't be judged. Don't condemn, and you won't be condemned. Set free, and you will be set free. Give, and it will be given to you: good measure, pressed down, shaken together, and running over, will be given to you. For with the same measure you measure it will be measured back to you."

– Luke 6:27-38 (World English Bible)

The Effects of Interest on Society

In *History of Money and Usury in America,* pages 33 to 34, Daniel Krynicki writes the following:

"Usury on simple loan contracts has always been the cause of economic oppression. And it still is. Usury makes a fungible[14] out of money. Without usury, money would merely be a medium of

---

13 An example of this would be a government fine.
14 Commodity.

exchange. What is really needed to eliminate barter? When we choose to use money as a fungible, we do it this way to satisfy our baser instincts like avarice, greed and lust. But without the usury in moneylending we open up an entirely new world of opportunity for everyone. Retail prices on goods and services would be more in alignment with what working people can afford. German Professor Margrit Kennedy claimed a full forty percent of prices of goods and services is comprised of usury. Almost all direct taxation would be done away with. The pages of the Bible thus show us a world of hope ahead, if we would only choose to look seriously at the very simple economic model God gave to Moses three and a half millennia ago. Please read carefully Leviticus chapter 25 **[10]**. As long ago as that was written, economic oppression was emphatically the reason the law against usury was committed to writing. That is why there should also be forgiveness on loans for disaster victims and unfortunate catastrophic illness. All these clauses were codified in the Mosaic Law. No doubt, even way back then, the overlooking Divine providence was a guiding light in the formation of Ancient Israel's constitution. Should we ignore, as did the ancient Israelites, these ways that were mapped out for them while we ourselves deliberate with our own initiatives to bring about good government?

"Gertrude Coogan's solutions in *'Money Creators'* somewhat mirror Stephen Zarlenga's model. But neither Coogan nor Zarlenga made mention of usury free lending. In fact Coogan, like Jefferson, approved of usury lending, as long as the lender has real capital to lend. This simply means 'book' or 'bank' ledger credit would be prohibited in her system. So Coogan's model would satisfy a good measure of the three needed elements; but she missed the target economically and Biblically on usury. She never did look into the deflationary effects of usury lending; nor did she realize that a federal agency could indeed administer usury free ledger credit to the people and business. The entire Biblical model can fund all public dues with direct legal tender currency emissions – Treasury Notes.

"Doctors and dentists purchase equipment for their practices, as do contractors and mechanics. All the principal plus interest they pay for their equipment, for the homes they live in and for the education of their offspring must be captured from the prices they charge to their customers.[15] If they all could obtain front capital usury free for whatever their life's needs are, would the retail prices they charge reflect the lowered costs? Usury free lending to all is one of the major elements for what is needed in an honest monetary system. It would also end economic oppression of the whole population. We would also be acknowledging that two thousand years ago one person with the name of Jesus Christ has been right all along.

---

15 Calculate your simple-loan here: http://www.amortizationtable.org/

"Therefore, until the time arrives in which the charging of interest on all simple loans is prohibited, and in which the authority to create our money is taken away from corporate anarchists who run the private banks, and thus restored back to the people through Congress with the outlawing of usury, this nation cannot be styled as something it never was: Christian."

In *Usury in Christendom: The Mortal Sin that Was and Now is Not,* pages 269 to 270 Michael Hoffman II writes the following:

"In the young and vibrant Roman Republic, circa 342 B.C. the *Lex Genucia* banned *all* lending at interest. Centuries later, in the era of the late Roman Empire as it rapidly decayed, the law defined usury only as interest in excess of 50%. It's no coincidence that in New Jersey at present the general usury limit is 50% for corporations. According to the American Bankers Association there are 26 states in the U.S. that have no limit on what bank credit card issuers can charge for interest rates. In a truly Christian nation this admission would be as shameful as a disclosure that someone had robbed an elderly couple or had an abortion.

"Equally despicable and Christ-dishonoring is the notion that Americans are affluent when the Shylock economy is humming along; the 'blessings' of capitalism etc. Yet, when the Shylock system is on the ascendant the majority of the people are in debt, because that debt is the engine of the overheated economy. Surrounded by electronic gadgets of every description and cars, boats, ATV's and snowmobiles, we think ourselves well off because our masters declare it to be so, when in fact, in terms of meaningful work, leisure time, stable marriages, lasting friendships and actual ownership (not mortgage) of land, we are but pompous paupers. Loneliness in America is a plague. Americans are friendless, loveless and adrift. Yet, for the past sixty years we have been told to be content that we live in the richest country in the world and share in the wealth. Yet, debtors are not rich. 'Debt is the worst poverty' (T. Fuller, 1732). The Cryptocrats who tell us otherwise are engaged in a civic magic, performing the work of making something metaphysically real even though its an illusion."

Results of Prohibiting Compound Interest[16]

---

16 While the current definitions of "usury" and "interest" are different, both words lead to the same consequences:
  I.   The transformation of money from a medium-of-exchange (a tool) to fungible (a commodity).
  II. The removal of more money from circulation than money that is inserted (deflation).
  III. The perpetuation of debt.

1. **Ends Money Scarcity.**

    Similar to interest on credit and loans, compound interest allows for more money to be taken out of circulation than what was put in (deflation). In *Interest and Inflation Free Money,* page 7, Margrit Kennedy provides an example where if a penny were deposited at the birth of Jesus Christ (between 6 and 4 BC) at five percent interest, it would be able to buy approximately 2,200 billion balls of gold in 1990.[17]

2. **Contributes to ending the Money Power.**

    In an article called *Debt Free Money alone does not solve Compound Interest,*[18] Anthony Migchels provides an example as to how the Money Power can take over the money supply of a nation through compound interest:

    "Let's say we implement Social Credit. The government prints money and the people spend it. The Money Power would open a number of banks on a full reserve basis, all credit backed by deposits.

    "During the first year it would acquire a fair bit of the new money. They would easily be able to do so: they could sell some of their gold or other assets. And they would have major income through, for instance, Big Business. It would use that income for their loan shark operation.

    "Let's say, for argument's sake, they obtain 10% of it's supply. They start lending at say 5%. Of this 5%, they use 2% for cost. The remaining 3% is profit, new capital, new deposits for their banks. After 1 year of lending, they control 13% of the money supply. After two years, 16.09%. After three years, 19.28%. After 10 years of lending, they would control 34% and after 20 years, 81% of the money supply.

    "Compound interest in operation."

Results of Prohibiting Interest on Credit and Loans

1. **Ends Money Scarcity.**

    The practice of charging interest removes more money from circulation than was put in by credit or loans. To support this claim, the author shall provide the following example:

---

17 You can read Margrit Kennedy's book *Interest and Inflation Free Money* here: http://userpage.fu-berlin.de/~roehrigw/kennedy/english/Interest-and-inflation-free-money.pdf

18 https://realcurrencies.wordpress.com/2012/01/05/debt-free-money-alone-does-not-solve-compound-interest/

If a borrower takes out a loan of $10,000, with a term of five years and an interest rate of six percent (which is within legal limits and considered ideal by Benjamin Franklin), then the lender will collect $11,599 at the conclusion of the contract. From this example, it is shown that the lender inserted $10,000 into the money supply, but withdrew $10,000 plus an additional $1,599. If one considers that on societal level, this example is being practiced (to various degrees), then it can be said that more money is being taken out of circulation than is being put in, which leads to deflation (money scarcity).

2. **Eliminates Excessive Taxation.**

The elimination of money scarcity (which results in currency inflation) and loan cost (interest on credit and loans; which results in price inflation, wage reduction, and unemployment) will lead to the end of financial destitution for a substantial amount of the citizenry, which, in turn, will lead to reducing the need for assistance from the Federal, State, and Territorial Governments. Due to reducing said assistance, the Federal, State, and Territorial Governments will no longer need as much revenue to finance their operations.

3. **Revitalizes Domestic Industry.**
   I. Due to interest no longer being passed on through the price of goods and services through loan costs, new goods and services can be created cheaply.
   II. The reduction in the cost of goods and services will not only lead to the creation of businesses, but it will also lead to the expansion of current businesses in the United States or increase in the number of businesses relocating to the United States from foreign nations.

4. **Reduces the Financial Burden of the Federal, State, and Territorial Governments.**

The revitalized economy will bring the unemployed back into the workforce, thus minimizing or eliminating the need for public assistance. (According to www.usgovernmentspending.com, the Federal Government will spend $1.127 trillion in 2017.) The cheapness of organic food and holistic medicine, the absence of emotional stress due to financial disparity, and more free time to exercise due to the elimination of the need to work multiple jobs, will allow the American People to become healthier. (According to www.usgovernmentspending.com, the Federal Government will spend $565 billion on healthcare in 2017.) The absence of interest upon loans and the reduction in the costs of goods and services will allow private businesses the ability to provide adequate retirement plans, thus eliminating the need for Social Security. (According to www.usgovernmentspending.com, the Federal Government spent $916 billion on Social Security in 2016.) The ability for one income to proficiently sustain a household will allow one spouse to remain at home and educate their offspring. (According to www.edu.gov, the Federal Government will spend $69 billion on education in 2017.) If we add these figures, which together come to approximately $3 trillion, to the estimated $5 trillion spent on the wars in the Middle East, we then come to almost half of the National Debt. (As of 2017, the National Debt of the United States is approximately $20 trillion.)

5. **Reduces Abortion, Penury, and Contraception.**[19]

   I. The reduction in prices and the increase in wages due to prohibiting interest, as well as the increase in employment opportunities due to ending money scarcity, this will end the financial destitution of a substantial amount of the citizenry, which, in turn, will lead to a decrease in the amount of abortions undertaken. According to the *United States Conference of Catholic Bishops,* 73% of abortions performed in 2005 were motivated by poverty.[20]

   II. The reduction in prices and the end of money scarcity will lead to couples no longer delaying or limiting procreation.

6. **Reduces the Division between Employers and Employees.**

   In *Digest of the Divine Law,* pages 96 to 97, Howard Rand writes the following:

   "Vested financial interests have been able to remain aloof from most labor disputes, making both management and labor assume that their difficulties are the result of the greed of the laborer or the selfishness of the employer, when in fact both are the dupes and slaves of a financial system which reaps both ends and the middle; always tending to bankrupt the employer[21] and withhold adequate compensation from the employee. Result: continued warfare between labor and management – each trying to save itself from the inevitable financial pressure from without by organizing against each other, both striving to control production, hours and wages, and blaming one another for their present plight.

---

19 In Canto XLV, Ezra Pound states interest on money is the cause of abortion, penury, and the usage of contraceptives.
20 http://www.usccb.org/about/pro-life-activities/respect-life-program/2014/poverty-and-abortion.cfm
21 In *Rape of Justice,* Eustace Mullins reveals that lawyers enact frivolous lawsuits in order to extort money from businesses. This too contributes to the financial disparity of employers.

"Let us always remember that the objective and end for both the employer and the employee are one. Each needs the other and both desire to receive from production a profit for their labor which should be a fair proportion of the value of that which is produced as the result of true collaboration between management and labor. This cannot become a practical actuality until there is a radical change in the entire monetary system to bring it into conformity with the Biblical standard of weights and measures as shown in the previous chapter."

Simply put, due to having to pay interest upon credit and loans (also known as "Loan Cost"), employers will have to lower wages, reduce or eliminate benefits, and or fire personnel.[22] This, in turn, leads to conflicts with their employees.

7. Reduces the Division between Landlords and Tenants.

In order to pay the interest upon the principal of the mortgage, the landlords increase the prices of the rent paid by tenants.[23]

8. Reduces the Division between the Races.
  I. Due to the fact that the elimination of money scarcity and loan cost will end the financial destitution of a substantial amount of the citizenry, said citizenry will be less susceptible to being manipulated by the plutocrats, who, in turn, use racism to distract the general public from class warfare.
  II. The newfound wealth achieved through the end of money scarcity, increased wages, and reduction in prices, will allow people of color to form their own communities away from each other and the white population. This will allow public officials (e.g. mayors and city councils), public services (e.g. emergency services and public schools), and private businesses to be of the same race, which, in turn, will lessen interracial violence and discrimination.
  III. The reduction in prices will allow all races to establish their own forms of media, which, in turn, can be used to counteract lies about or negative portrayals of themselves.

---

[22] The author does not deny the fact that greed on the part of employers contributes to low wages, reduced or discontinued benefits, and firing of personnel.

[23] Property Taxes and Opportunity Costs also contribute to high prices of rent.

9. Reforms the Christian Religion.

   I. The prosperity created by the revitalized economy will lead to either the end or reduction in the amount of proponents of the Prosperity Gospel, whom rely upon the disparity of the poor to flourish.

   II. The prosperity created by the revitalized economy will lead to more of the American People being able to either get health/medical care in general or better health/medical care in particular. This, in turn, will lead to the end or reduction of proponents of the Word-of-Faith Movement, whom rely upon the disparity of the sick and injured.

10. Ushers in Political Reform.

   I. The reduction in prices for goods and services will make campaigns cheaper, thus making it easier for new and or independent candidates to run for office.

   II. The wealth achieved through the end of money scarcity, increased wages, and reduction in prices will give the American People more money to donate to candidates. This, in turn, will allow more populists to either be contenders in elections or to remain in office without compromising themselves.

11. Protects Nature.

Interest makes the payment of debts more expensive than necessary. Thus, in order to obtain the money to pay said interest upon said debts, an individual (if they choose to not reduce wages, reduce or cut benefits, fire employees, take out more debt, raise prices, or sell or close their business) must create more goods and services than demanded; which, in turn, leads to a greater consumption of natural resources.

12. Restores National Identity.

In *Usury in Christendom: The Mortal Sin that Was and Now is Not,* pages 295 to 296, Michael Hoffman II writes:

"The memory and affections of the American people have been alienated from the land. The land is no longer a work of agrarian art for them, but an empty quarter that should be 'developed.' The deep disorder and psychic malaise afflicting America, which emerged into the open at Abu Ghraib prison in Iraq, where helpless Arab captives were made to strip naked, pantomime perverted sex acts and perform these acts for recordings on home video, is not just a matter of failure of American schools or parental upbringing in the home. Increasingly, American youth inhabit the landscape of nowhere; a cash-register geography that consists of the same string of fast-food joints and chain stores from Hoboken to Houston. In these canyons of sterility, displacement, rootlessness and deracination are pandemic. No Communist or Muslim raped America in this way. Her agrarian principles, her Biblical vision of the land as a sacred trust, were torn away and dumped into the refuse bin of history by the usury of the banks, the respectable Chamber of Commerce and the revered Fortune 500, amid the sybaritic complacency, conformity and Scripture-twisting of our 'ministers of the gospel."

Section Twelve:

"The United States shall not charge Interest or Fees or derivatives of the aforementioned on credit or loans to, as well as on debts of persons, corporations, or governments of foreign nations. In addition, no person residing; corporation created and operating; or financial institution created and operating in the United States or any place subject to its jurisdiction, shall charge Interest or Fees or derivatives of the aforementioned on credit or loans to, as well as on debts of persons, corporations, or financial institutions in foreign nations."

There are two reasons for the existence of Section Twelve of this amendment: 1.) To prevent the Federal Government, citizenry, corporations, and financial institutions from exploiting a loophole that can be found in Section Eleven of this amendment. 2.) To prevent the government, citizenry, corporations, and financial institutions of the United States from oppressing foreigners with interest and fees.

Section Thirteen:

"No person, corporation, or financial institution in the United States or any place subject to its jurisdiction shall be required by law to provide credit or a loan without obtaining collateral from the potential recipient of the aforementioned credit or loan."

The reason for the existence of Section Thirteen of this amendment is to prevent lenders from being forced the Federal Government to give free money to borrowers.

Section Fourteen:

"No person, corporation, or financial institution in the United States or any place subject to its jurisdiction, shall be required by law to return collateral to the recipient of credit or a loan, if the aforementioned recipient has not reimbursed the full amount of the money that was borrowed from the aforementioned person, corporation, or financial institution. In addition, this section shall not be so construed as to affect any recipient of credit or a loan before it becomes valid as part of the Constitution."

The reason for the existence of Section Fourteen of this amendment is to prevent borrowers from abstaining in the repayment of their debts to lenders.

Section Fifteen:

"Congress shall establish a bank. This bank shall provide deposit accounts to the residents of, corporations operating in, and residents of foreign nations aligned with the United States. In addition, this bank shall provide credit; loans; the ability to send or receive money; the ability to purchase or sell goods or services; and the ability to purchase or sell stocks of corporations to the residents of, corporations operating in, and residents of foreign nations aligned with the United States."

The reason for the existence of Section Fifteen of this amendment is to counteract potential attempts by the bankers to crash the economy of the United States (or the economy of the world) by refusing to provide credit, loans, and stock purchases/sales.

Section Sixteen:

"The right to put money in or withdraw money from; obtain credit or loans from; pay debts through; send or receive money through; purchase or sell goods or services through; or purchase or sell stocks of corporations through financial institutions other than the bank created by Congress, shall not be denied or abridged."

The reason for the existence of Section Sixteen of this amendment is to prevent the Federal Government from creating a monopoly over the banking system of the United States, which, in turn, can be used to oppress the American People.

Section Seventeen:

"With exception to income, nothing shall be taxed in the United States or any place subject to its jurisdiction. This tax shall be collected once a year. For Congress, this tax shall be collected on the fifteenth day of April. For the States and Territories of the United States, this tax shall be collected on the thirtieth day of April. For the Counties and Municipalities in the United States and its Territories, this tax shall be collected on the fifteenth day of May."

Excessive Taxation is Unnecessary

In *Digest of the Divine Law,* page 127, Howard B. Rand writes the following:

"With the revision of our present complicated system of government to conform with the Israel standard of administration the cost of operation would be materially reduced, while there would be no need of expenditures for relief – as the poor and needy would be provided for under the Israel economy. This answers those who question the sufficiency of the revenue for governmental purposes under the system of tithes. When to the above is also added the fact that there will be no interest to pay, or bonded indebtedness that absorbs so much of the government revenue today, an intolerable burden will have been removed."

Tax on Income

In *Digest of the Divine Law,* pages 92 to 94, Howard B. Rand writes the following:

"Property, both real and personal, is today subject to taxation. Our present method of taxing property has no relationship whatever to the earning power of the individual who is compelled to meet these assessments. The fact is we penalize men for improving their property and increasing the wealth of the nation and reward those who destroy values and allow their property to deteriorate. Thus through taxation the government fines the thrifty and industrious and rewards the shiftless.

"What is the remedy? It is a return to the Law of the Lord and its methods of taxation. Three principles must govern equitable taxation: 1.) Taxes must bear a definite relation to the income of the people and this relation must never be disturbed. 2.) In order to conform with this first principle, taxes must be levied against income only; leaving all property, both real and personal, free from tax levies and thus not subject to confiscation. 3.) The government must live within its income as a matter of sound business policy and remove forever the right to alter the tax principle. Under such conditions, government income is increased only by increasing the income of the people.

"The Israel system of taxation based upon the tithe complies with these principles. The tithe is a percentage of the income of the people and while the word tithe means a tenth of that income yet the returns are not limited to only a tenth of the income of the people. The fact is, the Bible sets forth three distinct tithes and when taken over a period of years amounts to about a fifth of a man's income or increase.

"Under the tithing system in Israel there were no tax levies made against property, either real or personal, but taxes were a percentage of a man's earnings or increase. When a man ceased to earn and failed to have any increase he paid no taxes! His possessions were free from confiscation and he could live and enjoy them though his earnings had ceased. Today we tax the possessions of a man and when the day comes that he ceases to earn, or have any profitable increase from his possessions, and is thus unable to meet these tax levies, his property is confiscated and he may end his days on the poor farm. This we call 'civilization.' But under the God-given system a man was protected in his holdings as old age approached and was free from fear of destitution and want.

"Because of national failure to recognize and keep God's laws of taxation we suffer with excessive levies against property and possessions (any levy against property itself is excessive) resulting in oppression and economic trouble. When the day comes that the nation keeps the law, then the vexatious problem of taxation will be solved forever and the administrators will live within their income which will be a percentage of the earning and increase of the people. The people will then be able to pay all the tithes without hardship, for God will pour out a blessing of real prosperity upon the nation when they keep His laws. Meantime the individual must tithe his increase and use it in the service of the Lord. He is obliged to set aside a tenth of his income for this purpose and in order to be eligible for the blessings as set forth by Malachi the prophet (Malachi 3: 10-18). Then when the nation observes the law the tenth will be increased to a fifth to include the tax levies for the support of the government."

Why no Property Taxes

In *Digest of the Divine Law,* page 111, Howard B. Rand writes the following:

"It was impossible to dispossess men of their inheritance under the law of the Lord as no taxes were levied against land. Regardless of a man's personal commitments he could not disinherit his family by being dispossessed of his land forever. Millions of people today have no inheritance in the land and are pauperized in a country where hundreds of thousands of acres of land lie idle and unused. Because taxes are levied against the land, instead of being levied against the increase from that land, men cannot afford to possess land. Through a system of debt that impoverishes the many and enriches the few the tendency has been to dispossess the many in our refusal to keep the law which states that 'ye shall not therefore oppress one another' and we penalize, through taxation, those who should inherit the land!"

Examples of why Property Taxes are Bad

- In 2006, Bennie Coleman, who completely paid off his mortgage in 1988, lost his home to the city of Washington D.C., due to missing a property tax payment of $134. The city of Washington D.C. would levy interest and fees upon the debt, increasing it to $317.[24]
- In 2019, Glen Kristi Goldenthal nearly lost her home to the government of Ocean Township, New Jersey, due to missing a property tax payment of 6¢. Interest placed upon the debt increased it to $300.[25]
- Thomas McRae, who was in hospice care after a battle with cancer, lost his home in Northwest Washington after missing a series of property tax payments that culminated in a debt of $1,025.[26]
- An elderly woman, who was combating Alzheimer's Disease, lost her home in Maryland due to missing a property tax payment of $44.79.[27]
- In 2018, Kevin Fair, who completely paid off his mortgage, lost his home to Scotts Bluff Country, Nebraska, after missing a series of property tax payments that culminated in a debt of $588.[28]

---

24 https://www.businessinsider.com/marine-veteran-foreclosure-2013-9
25 https://www.nbcnewyork.com/news/local/nj-homeowner-nearly-loses-her-house-because-she-owed-6-cents-in-back-taxes/2613724/
26 https://www.treasurenet.com/threads/left-with-nothing.374946/
27 Ibid.
28 https://apnews.com/article/home-returned-lawsuit-nebraska-e32c475557a3478b9ef15541b470cb31

Sole Tax – Response to Potential Rebuttals

As stated and shown above, if real property is taxed and a person ceases to pay, they will become homeless.

In regard to other taxes, the author states the following:

- If Goods and Services are taxed, then it will increase prices for consumers.
- If Imports (which overlap with Goods and Services) are taxed, it will create conflicts with foreign nations.
- Personal Property and Assets (e.g. Rental Properties and Estates of Inheritances) overlap with Real Property, Goods, and Services.

Results of Enactment

1. **Revitalizes Domestic Industry.**
    I. Similar to the elimination of interest, the elimination of the majority of the current taxes in the United States will lead to the lowering of the price (directly and indirectly) of goods and services. This, in turn, will lead to the creation of new goods and services (which will also be cheap in price).[29]
    II. The simplification of the tax system in the United States will not only lead to the creation of new businesses, but will also lead to either the expansion of businesses currently residing in the United States or the increase of businesses relocating from foreign nations to the United States.

2. **Reduces the Financial Burden of the Federal, State, and Territorial Governments.**

---

[29] Here is an example: CBS8 News of San Diego conducted a report on the price of gasoline in the State of California in 2022. According to their findings, $1.40 of an average $6.39 per gallon of gasoline was taxes (a combination of respective taxes instituted by all levels of government – from Municipality to the Federal Government).

However, this now leaves us with the question as to how much of the remaining $4.99 are taxes (and interest) that the oil companies, transportation companies, service stations, etc., passed onto the consumer and what is the actual true price of gasoline?

I. The elimination of most of the current taxes in the United States will further lower the price of goods and services – which will have already been lowered by the prohibition of interest. This will lead to both the creation of new and the expansion of current businesses, which will lead to a reduction in unemployment. The reduction in unemployment will lead to a reduction in the number of people on government programs (e.g. Welfare).

II. The reduction in the price of goods and services will increase the purchasing power of the dollar. This will not only reduce the operational costs of government programs, but it will permit more charity from private persons.

3. **Ends Abortion, Penury, and Contraception.**

Men and women, due to the reduction in the price of goods and services, will be able to afford either having children in general or expanding the number of children they have in particular.

4. **Ends the division between economic classes.**

The increase in the purchasing power of the dollar will improve the conditions of the lower and middles classes, which, in turn, will either lessen or eliminate their animosity towards the upper class.[30]

5. **Reforms the Christian Religion.**

The results are the same as stated in the chapter about Section Eleven of this amendment.

---

[30] Daniel Krynicki writes the following about individuals that demand the rich pay more than ten percent of their incomes: "It is a sad time, indeed, when individuals, who may look with envy at the vast wealth accumulated by shylocks and landlords across the past half-millennium, desire to invoke retribution upon them by imposing unfair tax schemes upon all. Our present state of wealth imbalance in the world occurred because all this wealth has been confiscated and accumulated by a few through our own disregarding of God's law against usury. We did it to ourselves. Vengeance belongs to the Lord; He will repay."

Section Eighteen:

"Congress, the States, the Territories of the United States, and the Counties and Municipalities within the United States and its Territories shall tax no more than ten percent of incomes. Congress shall only tax persons that reside in the United States and its Territories. States, Territories, Counties, and Municipalities shall only tax persons that have declared the aforementioned areas as their primary residence."

The Purposes of Taxation

Under this amendment, the reason as to why Congress would tax the American People will not be to raise revenue for the operations of the Federal Government, but to prevent the inflation of the money supply.[31]

Meanwhile, the reason as to why the States, Territories, Counties, and Municipalities tax the American People will be to prevent tyranny.[32]

Results of Enactment

1. **Changes Urban Planning and Development.**

    Due to no longer deriving tax revenue from the number of residential properties, but from the number people residing in their jurisdictions, municipalities will repeal single-family zoning laws. This will result in the creation of more Apartments, Townhouses, High Rise Buildings, and Duplexes.[33]

---

31 As explained in the chapter about Section Six of this amendment, Congress can finance the operations of all levels of government by creating the money needed to do so.

32 There are two examples of this that come to the mind of the author:
   I. In 2022, the State of Louisiana refused to grant funds to the city of New Orleans to update critical infrastructure, due to the latter refusing to enforce the former's abortion ban.
   II. In 2025, the Republican-controlled Congress, motivated by partisanship, entertained the idea of placing stipulations on disaster relief aid to the Democrat-controlled State of California.

These two examples alone serve as a warning to the potential danger of allowing one level of government to control another through the purse strings.

33 This will create more affordable housing for the American People and help the United States combat climate change by creating walking, cycling, and public transport oriented municipalities.

2. **Reduces the Financial Burden of All Levels of Government.**
    - The end of single-family zoning will lead to less infrastructure needing to built or repaired by all levels of government. (According to www.urban.org, State, County, and Municipal Governments, combined, spent $154 billion on roads in 2021.)
    - The elimination of the need to commute long distances will bring more people back into the workforce, which, in turn, will reduce the number of people on government programs.
    - The elimination of expenditures (e.g. vehicle maintenance, vehicle insurance, vehicle parking, purchasing gasoline, etc.) will lead to a substantial amount of the American People becoming wealthier. This, in turn, will reduce the number of people on government programs.

3. **Improves the Standard of Living.**

State, Territories, Counties, and Municipalities will strive to attract more tax revenue (people) by competing against each other to see who can enact the lowest taxes; reduce the most crime; create the most jobs; etc. This competition, in turn, will lead to inadvertently improving the standard of living for the American People.

Section Nineteen:

"No person that earns an income that is below the amount of income declared to be the threshold of poverty by Congress, shall be taxed by Congress. No person that earns an income that is below the amount of income declared to be the threshold of poverty by Congress, if they reside in the District that constitutes the seat of Government of the United States, shall be taxed by the aforementioned District. No person that earns an income below the amount of income declared to be the threshold of poverty by the State or Territory of the United States that they reside in, shall be taxed by the aforementioned State or Territory of the United States. And no person that earns an income below the amount of income declared to be the threshold of poverty by the State or Territory of the United States that they reside in, shall be taxed by the County and or Municipality that they reside in."

The reason for the existence of Section Nineteen of this amendment is to alleviate the plight of the poor in the United States.

Section Twenty:

"No person that is below the age of twenty-one years old, shall be taxed."

The reason for the existence of Section Twenty of this amendment is to assist young people in achieving financial independence from their parents or legal guardians.

Section Twenty-One:

"No person serving in the Armed Forces of the United States shall be taxed. No person that is honorably discharged from the Armed Forces of the United States due to receiving a severe permanent injury while serving in the Armed Forces of the United States, shall be taxed for the remainder of their life. No person that has been honorably discharged after serving twenty-five years[34] or more in the Armed Forces of the United States shall be taxed for the remainder of their life. And none of the aforementioned persons shall be deprived of their status of honorable discharge as punishment for a crime in the United States or any place subject to its jurisdiction, unless the aforementioned crime be treason against the United States, whereof they have been duly convicted."

There are three reasons for the existence of Section Twenty-One of this amendment: 1.) Reward Servicemen and Servicemen for their sacrifice. 2.) Improve the standard of living for low rank (E1-E7) military personnel.[35] 3.) Increase Enlistment.

Results of Enactment

1. **Reduces the Financial Burden of the Federal, State, and Territorial Governments.**

The elimination of taxation for active military personnel will permit them to save and invest more money for their future lives as civilians. This will reduce the number of veterans that are impoverished, which, in turn, will reduce the number of people on government programs (e.g.

---

[34] The author chose twenty-fives years because this section of the amendment was inspired by the Ancient Roman Empire. In the Ancient Roman Empire, an individual that served twenty-five years was rewarded with land and citizenship.

[35] According to ChatGPT, the approximated salaries (as of 2025) are:
- E1 – $29,000/year
- E2 – $31,000/year
- E3 – $37,000/year
- E4 – $44,000/year
- E5 – $52,000/year
- E6 – $61,000/year
- E7 – $82,000/year

Welfare).

2. **Strengthens National Security.**
    I. Due to the elimination of taxation for active military personnel, more citizens will enlist in the Armed Forces. This will increase the size of the United States Military.
    II. Due to the elimination of taxation for active military personnel, more citizens will enter the Armed Forces. This, in turn, will result in more civilians being trained to repel invasions and quash rebellions/insurrections.
    III. Due to the elimination of taxation for active military personnel and some veterans, there will be a reduction in the possibility of treason on their part against the United States.

Section Twenty-Two:

"No corporation created or operating in the United States or its Territories, shall be taxed."

The reason for the existence of Section Twenty-Two of this amendment is to prevent the incomes of corporations from being taxed, which, in turn, would result in said corporations passing off said taxes to consumers in the price of goods and services.[36]

Results of Enactment

This will create an influx of corporations from foreign nations into the United States, which, in turn, will create more jobs for the American People.

---

36 According to ChatGPT, there are less than a 1,000 Mega-Corporations in the United States. The remaining corporations in the United States are small and medium-sized businesses.

Section Twenty-Three:

"**No person below the age of eighteen years old, shall be permitted to marry or enter a cohabitation agreement in the United States or any place subject to its jurisdiction. In addition, no person shall be punished in the United States or any place subject to its jurisdiction for the act of refusing to marry, enter a cohabitation agreement, practice procreation, or adopt children.**"

There are three reasons for the existence of Section Twenty-Three of this amendment: 1.) To end child marriage in the United States.[37] 2.) To prevent single men and women from being coerced by the government into romantic relationships.[38] 3.) To prevent individuals, who are voluntarily childless, from being coerced by the government into creating or adopting children.[39]

---

[37] These are the parts of the United States that have outlawed child marriage (as of 2025): Washington, D.C.; American Samoa; U.S. Virgin Islands; Delaware; New Jersey; Pennsylvania; Minnesota; Rhode Island; New York; Massachusetts; Vermont; Connecticut; Michigan; Washington; and Virginia.

[38] The Ancient Roman Empire, through Lex Julia de Maritandis Ordinibus (also known as "Julian Law on Marrying Orders") and Lex Papia Poppaea punished (e.g. denied inheritances or "receiving legacies") individuals that were unmarried. This is an example of what the author seeks to prevent with Section Twenty-Three of this amendment.

[39] The Ancient Roman Empire, through, once again, Lex Julia de Maritandis Ordinibus (also known as "Julian Law on Marrying Orders") and Lex Papia Poppaea rewarded individuals that procreated and had multiple children (e.g. Jus Trium Liberorum). This is another example of what the author seeks to prevent with Section Twenty-Three of this amendment.

Section Twenty-Four:

"Marriage or a cohabitation agreement between persons of the same sex or gender; persons of different races, ethnicities, skin colors, national origins, creeds, or socioeconomic statuses; a non-disabled person and disabled person, if the aforementioned disabled person is capable; a non-cyborg and cyborg; a human and robot; two persons exclusively[40]; one person of the male sex or gender and multiple persons of the female sex or gender[41]; one person of the female sex or gender and multiple persons of the male sex or gender[42]; a group of more than two persons of one sex or gender[43]; and a group of more than two persons that is a mixture of sexes or genders[44], shall not be prohibited in the United States or any place subject to its jurisdiction."

There are two reasons for the existence of Section Twenty-Four of this amendment: 1.) To end the prohibition against bigamy in the United States. 2.) To protect people (e.g. Homosexuals and Practitioners of Interracial Romantic Relationships) in the United States from Christian and White Nationalists.

Where and Why the Opposition to Formal Polygyny Originated

Western Civilization's opposition to formal polygyny (i.e. one man marrying multiple women) began in the Ancient Roman Empire. The Ancient Romans outlawed formal polygyny to ease both the division of inheritances and the determination of citizenships. However, while formal polygyny was prohibited, informal polygyny (e.g. affair partners and sex slaves) was not prohibited.[45]

Polygyny – Response to Potential Arguments

---

40 The reason as to why the author mentions monogamy here is to protect future practitioners in case, if this amendment is enacted into law, they become a minority group in the United States.
41 Polygyny
42 Polyandry
43 Polyamory
44 Polyamory
45 In the Ancient Roman Empire, women, through Lex Julia de Adulteriis Coercendis (also known as "Julian Law on Adultery"), were prohibited from having extra-marital affairs, while men were not.

1. **"The legalization of polygyny will lead to inequality between the sexes."**

   Section Twenty-Four of this amendment will also legalize polyandry and polyamory. In other words, the legalization of polygyny will not create inequality between the sexes.

2. **"The legalization of polygyny will lead to the victimization of young and or vulnerable women."**

   If Sections Four, Eleven, Seventeen, Eighteen, Nineteen, Twenty, Twenty-One, Twenty-Three, Twenty-Seven, Twenty-Eight, Twenty-Nine, Forty, and Forty-Two of this amendment, along with other laws, are enforced by all levels of government, then there will be a reduced chance for the victimization of young and or vulnerable women.

3. **"The legalization of polygyny will lead to a conflict between the United States and United Nations."**
   I. Section Twenty-Four of this amendment, which legalizes polyandry and polyamory, is in compliance with General Comment Twenty-Eight by the Human Rights Committee (HRC) on Article Three of the United Nations Charter.
   II. Sections Twenty-Three and Forty-One of this amendment, which protects the rights of women concerning marriage, is in compliance with Article Sixteen of the United Nations Charter and General Recommendation Twenty-One.

4. **"The legalization of polygyny will reduce the number of viable women available to monogamous men and will create social unrest among single men."**

   Feminism[46] and the Manosphere[47] have already achieved this in our monogamous society.

---

[46] Here is how Feminism reduced the number of viable men for romantic relationships:
- **First-Wave Feminism** – Due to the fact that women were now able to financially provide for themselves, this lead to the number of men that were socially inept and or physically unattractive by societal standards, but capable in terms of intelligence, moral character, and financial standing to provide for a family, to be reduced in the mating pool.
- **Second-Wave Feminism** – Due to the fact that women were now able to prevent or eliminate pregnancies, this lead to the number of men that were not miscreants to be reduced in the mating pool.
- **Third-Wave Feminism** – Due to the fact that women were now able to practice non-traditional sexual decorum, this lead to the number of men that do practice traditional sexual decorum to be reduced in the mating pool.

[47] Here is how the Manosphere reduced the number of viable men for romantic relationships:

5. **"The legalization of polygyny will destroy the Nuclear Family."**

The author discusses in the chapter about Section Twenty-Five of this amendment about how the Judicial System of the United States has already achieved this in our monogamous society.

6. **"The legalization of polygyny will lead to an increase in the number of people on government programs (e.g. Welfare)."**
   I. Sections Four, Seven, Eight, Eleven, Seventeen, Eighteen, Nineteen, Twenty, Twenty-One, Twenty-Five, Twenty-Six, Twenty-Seven, Twenty-Eight, Twenty-Nine, Thirty, Thirty-Two, Thirty-Three, Thirty-Five, Forty-One, and Forty-Two of this amendment will reduce the number of people on government programs.
   II. Sections One, Six, and Eight of this amendment will make Congress able to completely finance government programs (including Welfare, SNAP[48], WIC[49], TANF[50], Medicaid, Section 8[51], and SSI[52]) without it being detrimental to the United States.

Polyandry and Polyamory – Response to Potential Arguments

1. **"The mixing of seed is wrong."**

This argument is obsolete due to the fact that modern technology (paternity tests) makes it possible to determine the parentage of a child in a polyandry/polyamory arrangement.

2. **"A woman cannot become 'One Flesh' with multiple men."**

This argument is invalid due to the fact that "One Flesh" is subjective. One Christian will argue that such a phrase is metaphoric, another will argue that it is literal. One Christian will argue that it is

---

Men that are formerly or currently promiscuous; currently overweight; creating (if not unintentional deadbeats or alienated parental figures) single mothers; laden with tattoos and or piercings; or currently indebted refusing to enter romantic relationships with women that are formerly or currently promiscuous; currently overweight; single mothers (if created by an intentional deadbeats or non-alienated co-parental figures); laden with tattoos and or piercings; or currently indebted.

48 Supplemental Nutrition Assistance Program
49 Women, Infants, and Children
50 Temporary Assistance for Needy Families
51 Housing Choice Vouchers
52 Supplemental Security Income (also known as "Social Security")

solely confined to the act of sexual intercourse, while another will argue that it encompasses the entire romantic relationship.

3. **"Polyandry/Polyamory is an affront to the natural order established by God."**

The response to this argument relies upon determining if the basis of this assertion is science or religion.

If the former, then the one who makes this assertion must contend with the fact that homosexuality, intersexuality,[53] polyandry, polyamory, and matriarchy have been found in nature.

If the latter, then the argument is invalid due to creeds, which determine what "natural order" is, being subjective.

The Distribution of Inheritances

These are the author's proposals on how to distribute inheritances among the practitioners of polygyny, polyandry, and polyamory:

1. **Polygyny**
    - **The Death of a Girlfriend/Wife**
        - If a woman dies without creating a will or trust, then any property that is lawfully obtained without the assistance of her boyfriend/husband or another girlfriend/wife prior to the cohabitation agreement/marriage, even if she later gifted that property to or jointly owned that property with her boyfriend/husband or another girlfriend/wife, will be inherited by her biological and or adopted children.
        - If a woman dies without creating a will or trust, then any property that is lawfully obtained without the assistance of her boyfriend/husband or another girlfriend/wife during a cohabitation agreement/marriage, even if she later gifted that property to or jointly owned that property with her boyfriend/husband or another girlfriend/wife, will be inherited by her biological and or adopted children.

---

53 Besides intersex animals, there are intersex humans. These humans are born with either chromosomes, hormones, gonads, or genitalia from both sexes.

- If a woman gifts property to a boyfriend/husband or another girlfriend/wife while she is alive and that boyfriend/husband or girlfriend/wife gifts said property to or jointly owns said property with another person, then that property will be returned to that woman's children upon her death if she dies without creating a will or trust.
- If a woman gifts property to a boyfriend/husband or another girlfriend/wife while she is alive and that boyfriend/husband or girlfriend/wife sells that property to another person, then said boyfriend/husband or girlfriend/wife will give a cash amount equivalent to the amount of money which said property was sold for to the woman's children upon her death if she dies without creating a will or trust.

- **The Death of Boyfriend/Husband**
  - If a man dies without creating a will or trust, then any property that is lawfully obtained without assistance of a girlfriend/wife prior to the cohabitation agreement/marriage, even if he later gifted that property to or jointly owned that property with a girlfriend/wife, will have its ownership determined by the casting of lots[54] among his girlfriends/wives.
  - If a man dies without creating a will or trust, then any property that is lawfully obtained without assistance of a girlfriend/wife during the cohabitation agreement/marriage, even if he later gifted that property to or jointly owned that property with a girlfriend/wife, will have its ownership determined by the casting of lots among his girlfriends/wives.

- **Simultaneous Deaths**
  - If a man and his girlfriends/wives die simultaneously without creating wills or trusts, the following will occur:
    I. The property of the women that was lawfully obtained without the assistance of their boyfriend/husband or each other will go to their respective children.
    II. The property of the man that was lawfully obtained without the assistance of his girlfriends/wives will have its ownership determined by the casting of lots among his children.

2. **Polyandry**

---

[54] The casting of lots should be officiated by a court of law.

The process in how to distribute inheritances in a polyandrous group will be the same as for a polygynous group, but the sexes/genders will be reversed.

3. **Polyamory**
   - **The Death of a Member**
     - If a member of a polyamorous group dies without creating a will or trust, then any property that is lawfully obtained without assistance from another member of the group (prior to or during this cohabitation agreement/marriage) will be inherited by their children.
     - If a member of a polyamorous group dies without creating a will or trust and doesn't have children, then any property that is lawfully obtained without assistance from another member of the group (prior to or during this cohabitation agreement/marriage), then ownership of their property will be determined by the casting of lots among said members.
   - **Simultaneous Deaths**
     - If all the members of a polyamorous group simultaneously die without creating wills or trusts, then the property that was lawfully obtained without the assistance of other members of said group will go to their respective children. For property that does not meet this criteria, ownership will be determined by the casting of lots among the children of all members of said group.

Medical Decisions

These are the author's proposals on how to appoint Healthcare Proxies for practitioners of polygyny, polyandry, and polyamory.

1. **Polygyny**
   - **Girlfriends/Wives**
     - If a woman does not declare a Healthcare Proxy before the need for one arises, then the Healthcare Proxy will be her boyfriend/husband. If the boyfriend/husband is unavailable, then one of the other girlfriends/wives will be selected to fulfill the role.

This selection will be determined by the amount of time each girlfriend/wife has been a member of this polygynous relationship.

- **Boyfriends/Husbands**
    - If a man does not declare a Healthcare Proxy before the need for one arises, then the Healthcare Proxy will be their first girlfriend/wife. If the first girlfriend/wife is unavailable, then another girlfriend/wife will be selected to fulfill the role. This selection will be determined by the amount of time each girlfriend/wife has been a member of this polygynous relationship.
- **Simultaneous Medical Incapacitation**
    - If a man and his girlfriends/wives are simultaneously incapacitated, then the Healthcare Proxy will be the eldest adult child of the polygynous relationship. If there is no such person, then the other options will be the following:
        - Family
        - Close Friend/Acquaintance
        - Attending Physician
        - Court-Appointed Guardian

2. **Polyandry**

The process in how to determine Healthcare Proxies in a polyandrous group will be the same as for a polygynous group, but the sexes/genders will be reversed.

3. **Polyamory**

If a person does not declare a Healthcare Proxy before the need for one arises, then it will be one of the following options:

- Family
- Close Friend/Acquaintance
- Attending Physician
- Court-Appointed Guardian

Section Twenty-Five:

"Palimony, Alimony, Child Support, or derivatives of the aforementioned, shall be prohibited in the United States or any place subject to its jurisdiction."

The reason for the existence of Section Twenty-Five of this amendment is to incentivize men to enter romantic relationships and procreate.

The Real Purpose of Palimony, Alimony, and Child Support

The real reason as to why palimony, alimony, and child support were created was to prevent members of the citizenry from becoming financial burdens to the government.

Title IV-D of the Social Security Act[55]

In 1975, the Federal Government created the Child Support Enforcement and Paternity Establishment Program. The purpose of this program was to prevent the bankruptcy of State Governments by both recuperating money spent on welfare recipients (custodial parents and their children) and deter the creation of new welfare recipients (custodial parents and their children).

Under this program, State Governments, who are tasked by the Federal Government to enforce and collect child support, obtain money through reimbursements, incentives, administrative fees, and arrears.

Why Title IV-D is Bad

Title IV-D of the Social Security Act is bad for the following reasons:
   I. During a trial for child custody, parents or legal guardians are suppose to be given two options by Family Courts as to how wage withholding is suppose to be conducted. The first option requires enrollment in the Title IV-D Program and the second option does

---

[55] Molly Olson, founder of the Center for Parental Responsibility, explains Title IV-D in a video, on her organization's YouTube Channel, called "The History of Title IV D Child Support Secrets".

not. Family Courts usually deceive (i.e. abstain from disclosing the existence of the second option) or coerce (e.g. threats of imprisonment for refusing the first option) people into selecting the first option.

II. State Governments, due to wanting to extract as much money as possible through reimbursements and arrears, have impoverished non-custodial parents and legal guardians through demanding high payments of child support. Meanwhile, due to wanting to obtain money through incentives and administrative fees, have endangered, indirectly damaged, or indirectly murdered children by either granting primary custody to the unfit parent or legal guardian[56] or preventing equal custody.[57]

Results of Prohibiting Palimony and Alimony

1. **Creates More Romantic Relationships.**
    I. Due to there being a reduction in financial incentives for engaging in romantic relationships, there will be a reduction in participants in dating and courtship that possess ulterior motives (e.g. gold diggers). This, in turn, will increase the number of people willing to date and or marry.
    II. Due to not being financially handicapped by palimony or alimony, people will be able to enter new romantic relationships.[58]

---

[56] The author has encountered testimonies online about how the Family Court awarded sole or majority custody of children to parents or legal guardians that were substance abusers, cohabitants with criminals (including child predators), and victims of severe mental illness. In addition, the author learned that, while the primary reason of the Family Court for these decisions were financially motivated (e.g. charging court fees to fit parents or legal guardians during each attempt to contest previous rulings concerning custody), the Family Court has been exercising discrimination based on the account of sex in their verdicts concerning custody of children.

[57] If Family Courts award sole or majority custody to the parents or legal guardians capable of financially supporting their children without the need of child support or enact equal custody of children between parents or legal guardians, then State Governments would not be able to profit from the Title IV-D Program. As a result, Family Courts rarely make such rulings.

[58] This will also lead to an increase in procreation.

2. **Creates Better Romantic Relationships**
   I. Due to knowing that they will not be tethered to their partner or spouse if the relationship fails, people will be emboldened to no longer accept subpar behavior and or treatment from their partner or spouse.
   II. Due to there being a reduction in financial incentives for discontinuing romantic relationships, there will be a reduction in people initiating unnecessary breakups.
   III. People, particularly those that aspire to be stay-at-home partners or spouses, will be more rigorous in their selection of potential romantic partners.

Results of Prohibiting Child Support

1. **Better Custodial Parents and Legal Guardians.**

   Due to State Governments no longer being able to financially exploit non-custodial parents or legal guardians, Family Courts will be more inclined to award custody of children to the parent or legal guardian that is not detrimental to the safety or well-being of said children.[59]

2. **Ends Corruption.**

   This section will end the Child Support Enforcement and Paternity Establishment Program.

---

59 The Family Courts may also be more inclined to award equal custody of children between parents or legal guardians.

Section Twenty-Six:

"The right of a person to divorce or terminate a cohabitation agreement in the United States or any place subject to its jurisdiction, shall not be denied or abridged. In addition, a person shall not be required to submit evidence of wrongdoing to a court of law in order to obtain a divorce or terminate a cohabitation agreement in the United States or any place subject to its jurisdiction."

There are two reasons for the existence of Section Twenty-Six of this amendment: 1.) To incentivize both men and women to enter romantic relationships and procreate. 2.) To protect Divorce, in general, and No-Fault Divorce, in particular, in the United States.

Why No-Fault Divorce is Good

1. **Prevents Corruption.**

    Prior to the enactment of No-Fault Divorce in the United States, married couples, with the assistance of the judicial system, would commit fraud in order to obtain divorces.[60]

2. **Prevents Endangerment.**

    No-Fault Divorce prevents recrimination, which either delays or eliminates the ability of an individual to obtain a divorce; even if that divorce is filed on justifiable grounds such as adultery, abandonment, and abuse.

    While recrimination, technically, is not the danger itself, it can lead to dangerous outcomes. For example, if a person files for divorce on the grounds of abuse, their abuser can issue a counter-claim (recrimination). This will either result in the case being prolonged or dismissed entirely. Both outcomes result in the abused remaining tied to the abuser. However, the former outcome will potentially result in either escalation of abuse, impoverishment of the abused[61], or one of the two parties of the case being murdered.

3. **Prevents Government Inefficiency.**

    Fault Divorce cases create backlogs in the judicial system.

---
[60] Judges and Lawyers would commit suborning perjury.
[61] This impoverishment is the result expenses garnered from the divorce trial.

Section Twenty-Seven:

"Any property obtained by a person, without receiving aid from their fiance or partner or obtaining it through committing an act of fraud or misappropriation towards their fiance or partner, prior to a marriage with the aforementioned fiance or cohabitation agreement with the aforementioned partner, irregardless if ownership of the aforementioned property is subsequently gifted to or jointly owned with their spouse or partner during the aforementioned marriage or cohabitation agreement, shall, upon divorce or termination of the aforementioned cohabitation agreement, be retained by the aforementioned person. In addition, any property obtained by a person without receiving aid from their spouse or partner during a marriage or cohabitation agreement, unless obtained through committing an act of fraud or misappropriation towards the aforementioned spouse or partner, upon divorce or termination of the aforementioned cohabitation agreement, irregardless if ownership of the aforementioned property is subsequently gifted to or jointly owned with their spouse or partner, shall be retained by the aforementioned person."

The reason for the existence of Section Twenty-Seven of this amendment, similar to Sections Twenty-Five and Twenty-Six, is to incentivize men to enter romantic relationships and procreate.

Results of Enactment

The results of this section will be similar to those stated in the chapter about Section Twenty-Five of this amendment – more and better romantic relationships.

Section Twenty-Eight:

"The right to obtain an abortion in the United States or any place subject to its jurisdiction, shall not be denied or abridged."

There are three reasons for the existence of Section Twenty-Eight of this amendment: 1.) Incentivize women to enter romantic relationships and procreate. 2.) To legalize abortion throughout the entire United States. 3.) To prevent future abortion bans.

Results of Enactment

1. **Creates Equality.**

Abortion bans only affect impoverished and politically powerless women. Wealthy and politically powerful women are able to circumvent said bans by either traveling outside of the areas where the bans have been enacted or using their influence to thwart the bans entirely.

2. **Creates More Romantic Relationships.**

Due to no longer fearing entrapment in terrible relationships, permanent injury to their bodies, or even outright death, women will be more willing to enter romantic relationships.

3. **Creates More Children.**

Due to no longer fearing entrapment in either terrible relationships or the raising of severely disabled offspring, permanent injury to their bodies, or even outright death, women will be more willing to have children.

Section Twenty-Nine:

"The right to obtain contraceptives in the United States or any place subject to its jurisdiction, shall not be denied or abridged."

There are two reasons for the existence of Section Twenty-Nine of this amendment: 1.) To incentivize the American People to enter romantic relationships and procreate. 2.) To prevent the banning of contraceptives in the United States.

Section Thirty:

"No Filial Responsibility or derivatives of the aforementioned, shall exist in the United States or any place subject to its jurisdiction."

The reason for Section Thirty of this amendment is to protect individuals from their abusive, estranged, or fiscally irresponsible parents or former legal guardians.

Section Thirty-One:

"The right of a terminally ill person, who is of sound mind and not below the age of eighteen years old, to choose to end their own life with the aid of a physician in the United States or any place subject to its jurisdiction, shall not be prohibited."

The reason for Section Thirty-One of this amendment is to protect individuals from suffering unnecessary long and agonizing deaths.

Section Thirty-Two:

"No corporation shall be anonymously created or anonymously operated in the United States or any place subject to its jurisdiction. In addition, no corporation shall be permitted to create or operate a subsidiary corporation in the United States or any place subject to its jurisdiction, that does not declare its purpose within or practice its purpose as expressed within its articles of incorporation or charter."

There are two reasons for the existence of Section Thirty-Two of this amendment:

1. **Prevents Criminal Activity.**

Former U.S. Senator Carl Levin, in his column *Bill would end corporate secrecy to fight terrorism, crime,* writes the following:[62]

"In August I led a bipartisan group of Senate colleagues in introducing a bill to combat terrorism, money laundering, tax evasion, and other wrongdoing aided by use of the corporations with hidden owners. This common sense bill would stop our states from forming about two million new corporations each year for unidentified owners, and instead require those applying to form a new corporation to list the owners behind it so that, if misconduct later occurred, law enforcement could track down the wrongdoers.

"The bill, which I introduced with sens. Chuck Grassley, Dianne Feinstein and Tom Harkin, has the support of the Federal Law Enforcement officers Association, the Fraternal Order of Police, the National Association of Assistant United States Attorneys, and the Society of Former Special Agents of the Federal Bureau of Investigation.

"Law enforcement groups support our bill because right now in the United States it takes more information to get a driver's license or to open a bank account than to form a corporation. Our bill would change that by requiring any state that accepts crime-fighting grants from the Department of Justice to add one new question to their existing incorporation forms, asking applicants to identify the company's true owners.

"That's it. One simple question. But it's an important one.

"Why? To begin with, we know some terrorists and criminals use U.S. Corporations to carry out

---

62 This article is available at: http://www.sourcenewspapers.com/opinion/guest-column-bill-would-end-corporate-secrecy-to-fight-terrorism/article_fd524d1c-d93e-582d-b47a-ba9aa2c80dc2.html

their activities. Viktor Bout, an arms dealer who was found guilty in November 2011 of conspiring to kill U.S. Nationals and selling weapons to a terrorist organization, used corporations around the world in his work, including a dozen formed in Texas, Delaware and Florida. It is unacceptable that Bout was able to set up corporations in three states and use them in illicit activities without ever being asked for his name. In another case, a New York company called Assa. Corp. owned a Manhattan skyscraper and in 2007 transferred about $4.5 million in rental payments to a bank in Iran. U.S. Law enforcement officers tracking the funds had no idea who was behind that corporation until another government disclosed that it was owned by the Alavi Foundation, which had ties to the Iranian military. In other words, a New York corporation was being used to ship millions of dollars to Iran, a notorious supporter of terrorism.

"U.S. Corporations with hidden owners have also been involved in financial crimes. In 2011, a former Russian military officer, Victor Kaganov, pleaded guilty to operating an illegal money-transfer business from his home in Oregon and using Oregon shell corporations to wire more than $150 million around the world on behalf of Russian clients.

"Shell corporations are also notorious for their role in health care fraud. One example involves an individual named Michael Huarte who formed 29 shells companies in several states including Florida, Louisiana and North Carolina, and used them to make fraudulent health care claims, bilking Medicare out of more than $50 million.

"In these and other cases, great law enforcement work eventually pierced the veil of corporate secrecy. But that's not always what happens. In October 2004, the Homeland Security Department's division of Immigration and Customs Enforcement identified a Utah corporation that had engaged in $150 million in suspicious transactions. ICE found that the corporation had been formed in Utah and was owned by two Panamanian holding corporations, all located at the same Panama City office.

"By 2005, ICE had located 800 U.S. Corporations in nearly every state associated with the same shadowy group in Panama, but was unable to obtain the name of a single person who owned any one of the corporations. ICE had learned that the 800 corporations were associated with multiple U.S. Investigations into tax fraud and other wrongdoing, but no one had been able to find the corporate owners. The trail went cold, and ICE closed the case.

"Our bill would not only help law enforcement in such cases, it would bring the United States into compliance with international standards requiring countries to obtain beneficial ownership information for the corporations they form.

"It would also make U.S. Domestic practices consistent with U.S. foreign policy. The fact that we have corporate secrecy right here in our backyard contradicts U.S. Efforts to end corporate secrecy offshore. All over the world, people are standing up and speaking out against shell corporations with hidden owners being used to commit wrongdoing. It is time Congress acted to ensure transparency in the formation of U.S. Corporations."

2. Contributes to reducing the influence of the Money Power.

In *History of Money and Usury in America,* page 19, Daniel Krynicki writes the following: "Another complication across the past one hundred years is found in the formation of holding or shell corporations. Since banking institutions have the authority to create new money, they then use this new money for lending to these holding companies and/or shell corporations which in turn obtain majority ownership in military defense contractors/manufactures and any corporation they deem will be profitable. Senator Carl Levin of Michigan recently introduced legislation that would prohibit the formation of anonymously owned corporations in the United States. Criminals have in recent years been using this method of escaping the scrutiny of law enforcement. How long of course have banking institutions been allowed to do this? Or more important, did the criminals learn of this trick from lawyers who worked for bankers?"

Section Thirty-Three:

"No corporation created and operating in the United States or any place subject to its jurisdiction, shall be required by law to achieve a profitable return on investment capital to stockholders."

The reason for the existence of Section Thirty-Three is to end Shareholder Primacy in the United States.

Results of Enactment

1. **Reduces Corruption.**

    Due to corporations in the United States no longer seeking to maximize the value of their stocks, there is less incentive for politicians to engage in Insider Trading.

2. **Improves Legislation.**

    Due to corporations in the United States no longer seeking to maximize the value of their stocks, there is less incentive for them to lobby for legislation that is harmful to the general public.[63]

3. **Protects Nature.**

    Due to corporations in the United States no longer seeking to maximize the value of their stocks, there is less incentive for them to either generate money by lobbying the government to permit harmful environmental practices or to save money by engaging in cost cutting measures that ultimately lead to harmful environmental practices.

---

63 This is a list of examples where Shareholder Primacy influenced legislation:
- Taft-Hartley (1947)
- Clean Air Act (1990)
- Nutrition Labeling and Education Act (1990)
- Graham-Leach-Bilely Act (1999)
- Commodity Futures Modernization Act (2000)
- Energy Policy Act (2005)

4. Ends Penury, Contraceptives, and Abortion.

Due to corporations in the United States no longer seeking to maximize the value of their stocks, there is less incentive to not grant their employees both adequate wages and benefits. This will end the financial destitution of a substantial amount of the citizenry, which, in turn, will lead to a decrease in couples delaying procreation, limiting procreating, or terminating their pregnancies.

Section Thirty-Four:

"No Minimum Wage or derivatives of the aforementioned, shall exist in the United States or any place subject to its jurisdiction. In addition, the wages or earnings of a person working in the United States or any place subject to its jurisdiction shall consist of nothing other than the money of the United States."

In regard to the first sentence of Section Thirty-Four of this amendment, there are three reasons for its existence: 1.) One reason as to why the Minimum Wage was enacted was to stop Non-White Tradesman and Laborers from undercutting their White Counterparts. 2.) The raising of the Minimum Wage negatively impacts small and medium sized businesses, but leaves mega corporations unaffected. 3.) The recent demand to raise the Minimum Wage is simply an attempt to counteract a consequence (high cost of living) of residing in our current monetary system. If the Federal Reserve System was eliminated, charging interest on money prohibited, taxation reduced, debts forgiven, and shareholder primacy ended, the cost of living would dramatically decrease in the United States.

In regard to the second sentence of Section Thirty-Four of this amendment, the reason for its existence is to prevent businesses from defrauding their employees by paying them in scrip.

Section Thirty-Five:

"No business in the United States or any place subject to its jurisdiction, shall be required by law to suspend operations during an epidemic or pandemic."

The reason for the existence of Section Thirty-Five of this amendment is to prevent a recurrence of what transpired during the COVID-19 Pandemic, which consisted of different levels of government across the United States impoverishing the American People through the forced closure of small and medium sized businesses, while simultaneously enriching the mega corporations by allowing them to continue operations unabated.

Section Thirty-Six:

"No copyright, patent, or derivatives of the aforementioned, shall exist in the United States or any place subject to its jurisdiction. In addition, no copyright, patent, or derivative of the aforementioned filed in a foreign nation, shall be enforced by a court of law in the United States or any place subject to its jurisdiction."

The reason for the existence of Section Thirty-Six of this amendment is abolish copyrights and patents in the United States.

Results of Enactment

1. **Creates Equality.**

Due to the absence of licensing fees and patent royalties creating a barrier to entry, the poor can compete with the rich.

2. **Enriches and empowers the United States.**

Under the current system of copyright (i.e. an person possessing exclusive rights to a work for the entirety of their lives and seventy years after their death), there is now a myriad of cases where up to two hundred years[64] worth of innovation, which can increase the power and general wealth of the United States, will be prevented from manifesting.

3. **Reduces cost for Federal, State, and Territorial Governments.**
    I. Due to there being no barrier to entry, small companies can compete with large Defense Contractors. This competition will reduce price gouging (if it exists), which, in turn, will reduce military spending by the Federal Government.
    II. Due to the absence of licensing fees, schools, universities, and labs can use material freely. This will reduce operation costs, which, in turn, will reduce spending on education and

---

[64] If an individual files a copyright when they are a toddler, lives to the age of 120 years old (it should be noted that some humans, such as Jeanne Calment, have lived passed this age), dies,, and then has an additional seventy years afforded to them after death, that almost comes out to 200 years of copyright ownership.

scientific research by the Federal, State, and Territorial Governments.[65]

III. Due to the abolishment of copyrights and patents, the judicial system in the United States does not have concentrate its resources on adjudicating cases of infringement.[66] This, in turn, will reduce spending by the Federal, State, and Territorial Governments.

4. **Preserves lost media.**

Due to the abolishment of copyrights, there will no longer be media trapped in copyright limbo. This, in turn, will prevent said media from being permanently lost to time.[67]

5. **Protects consumers.**

I. Due to the abolishment of copyrights and patents, there will be more competition in different areas of industry. This, in turn, will increase consumer protection from unnecessarily expensive, poor quality, and or artificially scarce goods and services.[68]

II. Due to the abolishment of copyrights, reviewers of goods and services will be protected from being silenced by the creator and or distributors of said goods and services. This, in turn, will protect consumers from unnecessarily expensive, poor quality, and or artificially

---

65 This will result in the following:

1. Under this amendment, the reduction in cost of operations for the Federal Government will lead to less inflation (stronger purchasing power for the dollar). Meanwhile, the States and Territories will either require less tax revenue to operate or they can redirect the extra tax revenue, which was obtained through the reduction in operation costs, towards an emergency fund or other areas that need attention (e.g. infrastructure).

2. The reduction in the cost to attend school or university will lead to more citizens becoming educated. This, in turn, will increase the power and wealth of the United States.

66 The abolishment of copyrights and patents will reduce the poor quality goods and services. This, in turn, will reduce the quantity of cases adjudicated by the judicial system concerning compensatory or punitive damages. This, in turn, will reduce the spending of the Federal, State, and Territorial Governments.

67 Not only does this prevent the permanent loss of knowledge, but, due to the creation of goods and services derived from media once trapped in copyright limbo, this also empowers (e.g. increases soft power) and enriches (e.g. creates new incomes for or increases then-current incomes of the citizenry, which, in turn, increases tax revenue) the United States.

68 An example of this that comes to the mind of the author is the war between internet pirates and streaming services.

scarce goods and services.

III. The abolishment of copyrights and patents will make it possible or easier for consumers to repair or maintain their purchased goods (e.g. electronics, appliances, and vehicles) and services (e.g. digital media) for either longer or indefinite periods of time.[69] This, in turn, will protect consumers from being impoverished due to having to continually purchase new goods and services.

6. **Protects the environment.**
    I. The abolishment of copyrights and patents will increase the pace of developing green energy and pollution cleanup technology.
    II. The abolishment of copyrights and patents will make it possible or easier for consumers to repair or maintain their purchased goods (e.g. electronics, appliances, and vehicles) for either longer or indefinite periods of time. This, in turn, reduces pollution.

---

[69] Right to Repair

Section Thirty-Seven:

"No person appointed as Justice to the Supreme Court of the United States, shall serve more than twenty-five years.[70] In addition, this section shall not be so construed as to affect the appointment of any Justice before it becomes valid as part of the Constitution."

The reason for the existence of Section Thirty-Seven of this amendment is to impose term limits on Supreme Court Judges.

---

[70] The author chose twenty-five years because he thought that a quarter of a century would be the best length of time for a Supreme Court Justice to serve.

Section Thirty-Eight:

"No solitary confinement of prisoners, shall be practiced in the United States or any place subject to its jurisdiction."

The reason for the existence of Section Thirty-Eight of this amendment is to end the practice of solitary confinement in the United States.

Section Thirty-Nine:

"Slavery or involuntary servitude as punishment for a crime, shall be prohibited in the United States or any place subject to its jurisdiction."

The reason for the existence of Section Thirty-Nine of this amendment is to complete the abolition of slavery in the United States.

Results of Enactment

This will end the Prison-Industrial Complex in the United States.

Section Forty:

"The right of citizens of the United States to vote shall not be denied or abridged by the United States, by any State, or by any Territory on account of conviction or imprisonment for a crime, unless the aforementioned crime is treason against the United States."

There are two reasons for the existence of Section Forty of this amendment: 1.) To protect the American People from disenfranchisement. 2.) To end the exploitation of prisoners by Public Officials via Prison Gerrymandering.

Section Forty-One:

"The right to borrow, loan, rent, own, sell, purchase, gift, bequeath, or inherit property in or outside of; to put money in, withdraw money from, send money to or from a financial institution in or outside of; to obtain credit or a loan in or outside of; to purchase goods or services in or outside of; to sell goods or services in or outside of; to work in or outside of; to obtain an education in or outside of; to serve in the Armed Forces of; to serve as a witness in a trial in a court of law in or outside of; to serve as juror in a court of law in or outside of; to a file a case in a court of law in or outside of; to invoke Habeas Corpus in; to create, enter, amend, leave, or terminate a contract in or outside of; to vote in or outside of; to hold public office in or outside of; to travel in, to, or from, the United States or any place subject to its jurisdiction, shall not be denied or abridged on the account of sex; gender; sexual orientation; race; ethnicity; skin color; creed; socioeconomic status; creed; marital status; childlessness or number of children possessed; disability, unless not capable; or national origin, unless it pertains to holding the office of President of the United States."

"You have heard that it was said, 'You shall love your neighbor and hate your enemy.' But I tell you, love your enemies, bless those who curse you, do good to those who hate you, and pray for those who mistreat you and persecute you, that you may be children of your Father who is in heaven. For he makes his sun rise on the evil and the good, and sends rain on the just and unjust. For if you love those who love you, what reward do you have? Don't even the tax collectors do the same? If you only greet your friends, what more do you do than others? Don't even tax collectors do the same? Therefore, you shall be perfect, just as your Father in heaven is perfect."

— Matthew 5: 43-48 (World English Bible)

There are two reasons for the existence of Section Forty-One of this amendment: 1.) To make civil rights legislation permanent in the United States. 2.) To protect the American People from Christian and White Nationalists.

Section Forty-Two:

"The manufacture, sale, purchase, possession, or transportation of cannabis, psilocybin mushrooms, or byproducts of the aforementioned within, the importation thereof into, or the exportation thereof from the United States or any place subject to its jurisdiction, shall not be prohibited."

The reason for the existence of Section Forty-Two of this amendment is to legalize cannabis and psilocybin "magic" mushrooms throughout the entire United States.[71]

---
[71] Both drugs have either been legalized or decriminalized by lower levels of government. .

Section Forty-Three:

"Sex work and prostitution shall not be prohibited in the United States or any place subject to its jurisdiction. In addition, no person below the age of eighteen years old, shall be permitted to practice sex work or prostitution in the United States or any place subject to its jurisdiction."

In regard to the first sentence of Section Forty-Three of this amendment, there are two reasons for its existence: 1.) To protect sex work that is currently legal in the United States from being banned by Christian Nationalists. 2.) To legalize prostitution in the United States.[72]

In regard to the second sentence of Section Forty-Three of this amendment, the reason as to why it exists is that the author did not want to leave the age selection to the States and Territories.[73]

Stipulations for Prostitutes

These are stipulations that the author thinks need to be enacted for any person that wishes to work as a prostitute in the United States:

1. They need to be licensed and registered in a database.
2. They need to be educated in the following:
   - Reproductive Health and Sexual Education
   - Recognizing and Responding to Abuse
   - Drug Recognition and Identification
   - Reading, Writing, and Negotiating Contracts
   - Personal Finance
3. They need to be trained in the following:
   - Martial Arts
   - Weapons Usage (e.g. Pepper Spray, Tasers, Blades, and Firearms)
   - First Aid
   - Cardiopulmonary Resuscitation (CPR)
   - S.E.R.E. (Survival, Evasion, Resistance, and Escape)

---

[72] This is to help both current and future sexually frustrated people in our society.
[73] The author feared the possibility that some of the States, since they permit child marriage, would permit child sex workers.

4. They need to perform routine health/medical checkups between every three to six months.[74]

---

[74] The author thinks that eye, ear, and psychological evaluations should be included in these checkups.

Section Forty-Four:

"Conscription into the Armed Forces of the United States, including during times of rebellion, insurrection, or invasion, shall be prohibited."

There are two reasons for the existence of Section Forty-Four of this amendment: 1.) To abolish Selective Service. 2.) To prevent the creation of a future military draft.

Section Forty-Five:

"Congress shall have the power to enforce this article by appropriate legislation."

These are the following ways in which Congress can, but is not limited to, enforce this amendment:

1. Create and enforce legislation that punishes entities in the United States that refuse to forgive debts.
2. Create and enforce legislation that punishes entities in the United States that, upon the first debt forgiveness, attempt to seize collateral.
3. Create and enforce legislation that punishes entities (lenders) that attempt to defraud other entities (borrowers) of their collateral after debts have been successfully repaid before debt forgiveness.
4. Create and enforce legislation that punishes entities (borrowers) that attempt to defraud other entities (lenders) of their collateral in a court of law after failing to repay debts before the debt forgiveness.
5. Create and enforce legislation that removes Federal Reserve Notes (digital and physical) from circulation in the global economy.
6. Create and enforce legislation that resumes the production of United States Notes and injects said Notes (digital and physical) into circulation in the global economy.
7. Create and enforce legislation that abolishes the Petrol Dollar.
8. Create and enforce legislation that punishes entities in the United States that charge interest.
9. Create and enforce legislation that punishes entities in the United States that charge fees on credit, loans, and debts.
10. Create and enforce legislation that restructures the Federal Reserve System into the bank that is discussed in Section Fifteen of this amendment. In addition, this legislation also does the following:
    - Create Debit Cards, Credit Cards, and Checks for people that use this bank.
    - Create a Website and Mobile App for people that use this bank.
    - Create more physical locations of this bank across the United States and its Territories.
    - Create more physical locations of this bank outside of the United States.

11. Create and enforce legislation that punishes entities in the United States that refuse to accept tangible forms of the money of the United States to pay for goods, services, and debts.
12. Create and enforce legislation that punishes States, Territories, Counties, and Municipalities that attempt to enact taxes that violate Section Seventeen of this amendment.
13. Create and enforce legislation that punishes States, Territories, Counties, and Municipalities that attempt to collect taxes more than once a year as discussed in Section Seventeen of this amendment.
14. Create and enforce legislation that punishes States, Territories, Counties, and Municipalities that attempt to enact income taxes greater than what is permitted in Section Eighteen of this amendment.
15. Create and enforce legislation that punishes States, Territories, Counties, and Municipalities that attempt fraud against persons by claiming that they declared the aforementioned areas as primary residence.
16. Create and enforce consequences towards States, Territories, Counties, and Municipalities that permit child marriage.
17. Create and enforce legislation that punishes entities in the United States that violate the rights of persons that are single and or childless.
18. Create and enforce legislation that punishes entities that violate the rights of persons that practice homosexuality, non-monogamy, or interfaith or interracial relationships.
19. Create and enforce legislation that punishes States, Territories, Counties, and Municipalities that continue to enforce palimony, alimony, or child support.
20. Create and enforce legislation that punishes States, Territories, Counties, and Municipalities that enact derivatives of palimony, alimony, or child support.
21. Create and enforce legislation that punishes entities that violate the rights or safety of persons that seek to obtain an abortion in the United States.
22. Create and enforce legislation that punishes entities that violate the rights or safety of persons that seek to obtain contraceptives.
23. Create and enforce legislation that punishes States, Territories, Counties, and Municipalities that continue to enforce filial responsibility.
24. Create and enforce legislation that punishes States, Territories, Counties, and Municipalities that attempt to enact derivatives of filial responsibility.

25. Create and enforce legislation that punishes entities that violate the rights of terminally ill persons that choose to end their own lives with the aid of physicians.
26. Create and enforce legislation that punishes entities that anonymously own or attempt to anonymously establish corporations in the United States or its Territories.
27. Create and enforce legislation that punishes shareholders that attempt to sue a corporation in a court of law for failing to achieve a profitable return on their capital investment.
28. Create and enforce legislation that punishes States, Territories, Counties, and Municipalities that continue to enforce a minimum wage.
29. Create and enforce legislation that punishes States, Territories, Counties, and Municipalities that enact derivatives of minimum wage.
30. Create and enforce legislation that punishes States, Territories, Counties, and Municipalities that make businesses suspend operations during a epidemic or pandemic.
31. Create and enforce legislation that releases all copyrights and patents filed in the United States to the general public for free use.
32. Create and enforce legislation that repeals the Invention Secrecy Act of 1951.
33. Create and enforce legislation that punishes States, Territories, Counties, and Municipalities that practice slavery or involuntary servitude.
34. Create and enforce legislation that releases prisoners from solitary confinement.
35. Create and enforce legislation that punishes States, Territories, Counties, and Municipalities that violate the voting rights of current or former criminals or prisoners.
36. Create and enforce legislation that expunges prisoners across the United States of charges pertaining to possession or distribution of cannabis, psilocybin mushrooms, or their byproducts.
37. Create and enforce legislation that establishes a license and database for persons that desire to practice prostitution in the United States.
38. Create and enforce legislation that punishes prostitutes, if they are still practicing in the United States, that do not keep their licenses current.
39. Create and enforce legislation that punishes prostitutes, if they are still practicing in the United States, that do not keep their training current.
40. Create and enforce legislation that punishes prostitutes, if they are still practicing in the United States, that do not keep their health (mental, physical, and reproductive) exceptional.
41. Create and enforce legislation that protects prostitutes from clientele that refuse to disclose

recent medical history.

Free-Enterprise vs. Capitalism[75]

• "...serves widespread economic freedom based on pure human merit." • "...must be inventive and creative in every opportunity (out of necessity)." • "...demands diversity...differing perspectives, continuous experimentation and improvement. But strives to create a long-term harmony for everybody, not short-term, unsustainable domination periods for a few." • Utilizes the natural resources in the local community, which equates to an improved standard of living (e.g. less spending, nutritious organic food, etc.) • Logical, inclusive, "creative, inventive, and fun." • "...wants to create more enterprise, more utility, more value, more toys, more achievement. Not More and even More Paper for lazy, lying, untalented, hateful, and insidious [men] who lurk among the population." • "...needs fair public governance to keep the play free." • "...has everything to do with new progress to change the status quo." • "...needs peace in order to communicate, sell, and grow itself."	• "Favors the few." • "...serves the infinite dominance of a few capital holders." • "...has to either usurp or suppress human merit when it needs to, in order to develop and protect its interests. As such, it arises from and contributes to sick, twisted, unproductive, and unsustainable souls." • "...not a sustainable set of methods. It's plunder in short. Its aims are socio-pathological." (e.g. International Bankers propose public works, but the common people finance and construct them.) • Creates waste and decadence. • Focuses upon wealth accumulation and "promises privilege, elitism, exclusivity, dominance, secrecy, etc." • "...needs unbalanced, skewed government to help them steal other people's wealth and stop them from rising up to threaten their position." • "...rarely has enthusiasm for anything new to change the status quo." • Sole justification for its existence is to granting the population the false hope of joining their exclusivity. • "...needs war in order to create demand for big capital layouts, profiting from that."

---

75 https://www.linkedin.com/pulse/organic-economy-vs-fake-paper-metin-ozsavran?trk=mp-reader-card

Four Hour Workday

In *Social Credit:An Impact,* Ezra Pound proposes a way to create more jobs for people under an interest-free monetary system and that is Four Hour Workdays.

According to Ezra Pound, the following must be done:

1. Eight hour workdays are reduced to four hour work days.
2. Labor laws prohibit people from working overtime at their jobs. If they desire to make more money, they must do another job.[76]

Results of Enactment

1. **Reduces the Financial Burden on the Federal, State, and Territorial Governments.**

Diving the workday would create more employment, thus reducing the amount of people in poverty and reliant on government programs.

2. **Improves the American People.**

Reduction in the amount of time devoted to work would minimize stress and exhaustion, which would improve the mental, physical, and relational well-being of the American People.[77]

3. **Improves Goods and Services.**

Reduction in the amount of time devoted to work would minimize boredom, which, in turn, would make employees more alert and happy. This alertness would create better goods and workplace safety, while happiness would lead to more tasks completed and customers obtained.[78]

---

76 Ezra Pound suggested that the second job of a person should be related to the arts.
77 This would contribute to reducing the financial burden of the government in the following ways:
　1. Reducing the number of impoverished people reliant on government programs, due to some marriages not ending in divorce because of workplace stress and exhaustion.
　2. Reducing the number of criminals in the United States due to creating more nurturing home environments for children because their parents are mentally present due to the absence of workplace stress and exhaustion.

78 Positive interaction and efficiency created by employees being happy will result in businesses getting more customers.

Federal Reserve Act: Transition Period

Daniel Krynicki writes in his correspondence with the author:

"People, who have struggled all their lives to accumulate savings in a hostile monetary system, have no recourse at recapturing a life long battle carving out a niche for their retirement and children's future.

"It is the bonds issued by the Treasury that should be repudiated, not the Federal Reserve Notes kept locked up in the savings of personal and familial banking accounts, or in their pockets, or buried in the ground.

"Why not a period in which individual citizens can redeem their Federal Reserve Notes that are held as 'Savings,' in exchange for the new legal tender notes? Some individuals have saved a portion of their earnings for an education, an automobile or home purchase. Others have placed some of their earnings into a '401k Savings' plan or an 'IRA Savings' account for retirement. But to forego the administrative nightmare of a redemption period, I have suggested that even though no new Federal Reserve Notes will henceforth be issued, those Federal Reserve Notes that exist in the accounts and pockets of private individuals, or those buried in a PVC pipe underground, should be fully interchangeable with the new Treasury Notes.

"Numismatists, who have an affection for old money for their collections, would give national attention to such clause. If you recall from history, some of Lincoln's Greenbacks are held in such collections to this day. The Greenbacks circulated among the people as money for quite a few years after their issue was stopped. Thus, there is really no need to penalize the people with such clauses.

"Redemption is the release of debt. We are striving here to make it a law that such redemption from debt bondage targets the shylocks, not the people. We do this by repudiating the interest bearing bonds that the Treasury has issued and the outlawing of usury, not by repudiating the currency notes in circulation. This way no interest makes its way into the accounts of the money-power, due to there being no bonds upon which to pay either interest or principal."

Bible Verses on Interest/Usury

"If you lend money to any of my people with you who is poor, you shall not be to him as a creditor. You shall not charge him interest."

– Exodus 22: 25 (World English Bible)

"If your brother has become poor, and his hand can't support himself among you, then you shall uphold him. He shall live with you like an alien and a temporary resident. Take no interest from him or profit; but fear your God, that your brother may live among you. You shall not lend him your money at interest, nor give him your food for profit."

– Leviticus 25: 35-37 (World English Bible)

"You shall not lend on interest to your brother: interest of money, interest of food, interest of anything that is lent on interest. You may charge a foreigner interest; but you shall not your brother interest, that Yahweh your God may bless you in all that you put your hand to, in the land where you go in to possess it."

– Deuteronomy 23: 19-20 (World English Bible)[79]

"I was very angry when I heard their cry and these words. Then I consulted with myself, and contended with the nobles and the rulers, and said to them, 'You exact usury, everyone of his brother.' I held a great assembly against them. I said to them, 'We, after our ability, have redeemed our brothers the Jews that were sold to the nations; and would you even sell your brothers, and should they be sold to us?' Then they held their peace, and found not a word to say. Also I said, 'The thing that you do is not good. Shouldn't you walk in the fear of our God, because of the reproach of the nations our enemies? I likewise, my brothers and my servants, lend them money and grain. Please let us stop this usury. Please restore to them, even today, their fields, their vineyards, their olive groves, and their houses, also the

---

[79] Daniel Krynicki writes in his correspondence with the author: "This has been nullified in Luke 6: 27-36. The 'Foreigner' stated in this passage is an *outlandish* or *hostile* Foreigner. Now, in Luke Chapter Six, we are commanded by Jesus Christ to '...love [our] enemies, and do good, *and lend, expecting nothing back*.' This context is affirmed in the Hebrew Masoretic and Greek Septuagint translations of the Old Testament. Scholarship provided to us by 19th Century Bible Linguist James Strong makes, with impetus, this assertion."

hundredth part of the money, and of the grain, the new wine, and the oil, that you are charging them."

— Nehemiah 5: 6-13 (World English Bible)

"Yahweh, who shall dwell in your sanctuary?
Who shall live on your holy hill?
He who walks blamelessly and does what is right,
and speaks truth in his heart;
he who doesn't slander with his tongue,
nor does evil to his friend,
nor casts slurs against his fellow man;
in whose eyes a vile man is despised,
but who honors those who fear Yahweh;
he who keeps an oath even when it hurts, and doesn't change;
he who doesn't lend out his money for usury,
nor take a bribe against the innocent.
He who does these things shall never be shaken."

— Psalm 15: 1-5 (World English Bible)

"Yahweh's words came to me again, saying, 'What do you mean, that you use this proverb concerning the land of Israel, saying, 'The fathers have eaten sour grapes, and the children's teeth are set on edge'? 'As I live,' says the Lord Yahweh, 'you shall not use this proverb any more in Israel. Behold, all souls are mine; as the soul of the father, so also the soul of the son is mine. The soul who sins, he shall die.
But if a man is just,
and does that which is lawful and right,
and has not eaten on the mountains,
hasn't lifted up his eyes to the idols of the house of Israel,
hasn't defiled his neighbor's wife, hasn't come near a woman in her impurity,
and has not wronged any,
but has restored to the debtor his pledge,

has taken nothing by robbery,

has given his bread to the hungry,

and has covered the naked with a garment;

he who hasn't lent to them with interest,

hasn't taken any increase from them,

who has withdrawn his hand from iniquity,

has executed true justice between man and man,

has walked in my statutes,

and has kept my ordinances,

to deal truly;

he is just,

he shall surely live,' says the Lord Yahweh.

If he fathers a son who is a robber who sheds blood, and who does any one of these things, or who does not do any of those things, but even has eaten at the mountain shrines, and defiled his neighbor's wife, has wronged the poor and needy, has taken by robbery, has not restored the pledge, and has lifted up his eyes to the idols, has committed abomination, has lent with interest, and has taken increase from the poor; shall he then live? He shall not live. He has done all these abominations. He shall surely die. His blood will be on him. Now, behold, if he fathers a son, who sees all his father's sins, which he has done, and fears, and does not such like;

who hasn't eaten on the mountains,

hasn't lifted up his eyes to the idols of the house of Israel,

hasn't defiled his neighbor's wife,

hasn't wronged any,

hasn't taken anything to pledge,

hasn't taken by robbery,

but has given his bread to the hungry,

and has covered the naked with a garment;

who has withdrawn his hand from the poor,

who hasn't received interest or increase,

has executed my ordinances,

has walked in my statutes;

he shall not die for the iniquity of his father. He shall surely live. As for his father, because he cruelly oppressed, robbed his brother, and did that which is not good among his people, behold, he will die in his iniquity."

– Ezekiel 18:1-18 (World English Bible)

Prescriptive Bible Verses on Polygyny/Polygamy[80]

"If a man sells his daughter to be a female servant, she shall not go out as the male servants do. If she doesn't please her master, who has married her to himself, then he shall let her be redeemed. He shall have no right to sell her to a foreign people, since he has dealt deceitfully with her. If he marries her to his son, he shall deal with her as a daughter. If he takes another wife to himself, he shall not diminish her food, her clothing, and her marital rights. If he doesn't do these three things for her, she may go free without paying any money."

— Exodus 21:7-11 (Word English Bible)

"You shall not take a wife in addition to her sister, to be a rival, to uncover her nakedness, while he sister is still alive."

— Leviticus 18:18 (World English Bible)

"If a man has two wives, the one beloved and the other hated, and they have borne him children, both the beloved and the hated, and if the firstborn son is hers who was hated, then it shall be, in the day that he causes his sons to inherit that which he has, that he may not give the son of the beloved the rights of the firstborn; but he shall acknowledge the firstborn, the son of the hated, by giving him a double portion of all that he has; for he is the beginning of his strength. The right of the firstborn is his."

— Deuteronomy 21:15-17 (World English Bible)

"Nathan said to David, 'You are the man! This is what the Lord, the God of Israel, says: 'I anointed you king over Israel, and I delivered you out of the hand of Saul. I gave you your master's house and your master's wives into your bosom, and gave you the house of Israel and of Judah; and if that would have been too little, I would have added to you many more such things...'"

---

[80] The author recommends the literary works written by Pete Rambo – *Jesus' Perspective on Polygyny* and *Paul's Perspective on Polygyny*. Both essays address the common arguments that Christians pose against polygyny/polygamy.

— 2 Samuel 12:7-8 (World English Bible)

Why this Amendment and the Future Fight

1. **Why this system?**

    In *Digest of the Divine Law,* pages 81 and 82, Howard B. Rand writes:

    "*Socialism* proposes to change these conditions by state ownership and control of the means of production. It aims to secure the reconstruction of society, increase wealth and bring about a more equitable distribution of the products of labor through public collective management of all industries. *Communism* is a social system in which there is community of goods. It calls for the abolition of all private property (by force of violence, if necessary) and the absolute control by the community in all matters pertaining to labor, religion and social relationships. *Capitalism* is a system of competition that favors the concentration of capital (resources or wealth employed in or available for production) in the hands of a few. Thus in these three systems of man there is in capitalism destructive competition with poverty in the midst of plenty; in socialism, state control and the destruction of private industry; in communism, community of goods and destruction of private ownership.

    "In operation, the system of capitalism has proved wanting and has been unable to establish an equitable distribution of wealth and bring prosperity and happiness to all men everywhere, while during its activity poverty has grown in the midst of plenty. Because this has been so, the advocates of socialism and communism have pointed to the failure of the capitalistic methods as reasons why their particular brand of social order should be established in its place. But the continuation of capitalism, the substitution of socialism, or the adoption of communism will not cure the economic ills of mankind."

2. **What lies ahead?**

    In *Digest of the Divine Law,* pages 208 and 209, Howard B. Rand writes:

    "Opposition to the institution of sound money and a return to a balanced monetary system, with the supply expanding and contracting in accord with demand, will meet with violent objection as all those who have approached the solution of this problem well know. Powerful interests which have made the present system yield them billions of dollars in surreptitious profits are not going to let the people or their Congress change the system without a fight.. They are opposed to sound money and an adequate credit system where sterling character and enterprise will enable men to secure credit and carry on successful business transactions free from fear of confiscation and destruction of their possessions by periodic depressions engineered by financial parasites.

"But until, as a nation, we return to a monetary system based on a stable unit of value, allowing the supply to expand and contract in accord with the demand to keep the value constant, there can be no economic peace nor freedom from destitution and want in our land. Those who are responsible for the present situation and its continuation are greater enemies of our nation than even the directors, evil as they are. "True wealth is represented in our possessions. And a true standard, an *unvarying unit of value for measuring that wealth,* is essential if our people are to be prosperous, contented, happy, and free."

Conclusion

In this conclusion, the author will address potential arguments and or assertions made against him:

1. **"You advocate 'Free Money'."**

    While the author advocates for credit and loans to be interest-free, he did not state that credit and loans would be administered freely. The author advocates that lenders demand collateral from borrowers if the latter wishes to obtain credit or loans from the former.

2. **"If you don't want to pay interest, then, instead of borrowing money, just save it up."**
    I. Due to currency inflation and price inflation (loan costs), the savings of an individual will be made less valuable over time.
    II. Interest does not solely affect the recipients of credit and loans. Some of the recipients, who are business owners, will either raise the price of goods and services; lower wages; reduce or eliminate benefits; and fire employees. In other words, interest affects more people than credit and loan recipients.
    III. If an individual is without sufficient funds and a sudden emergency arises (e.g. appliance failure; catastrophic illness; natural and or man-made disaster; etc.) and they do not have wealthy family or friends to rely upon, then they may have to take out credit or loans in order to contend with said emergency.
    IV. Due to an individual having to save up money instead of taking out credit or a loan, they may miss the "window of opportunity" to make their idea a success.

3. **"Interest is necessary to combat inflation."[81]**

    Interest is a reason as to why currency and price inflation exist. The government must issue more money than is necessary in order to satisfy the interest upon the previous loans from both public and private entities, as well as to compensate the deflation created by compound interest and interest upon credit and loans to the citizenry.

    Meanwhile, the interest upon credit and loans to the citizenry leads to a rise in the price of

---

81 This is known as the "Time Value Hoax" and is addressed by Anthony Migchels in this article: https://realcurrencies.wordpress.com/2013/12/11/rationalizing-usury-the-time-value-hoax/

goods and services.

4. **"Interest is fine as long as it doesn't outpace the issuing of currency."**
   I. Due to interest being deflationary, currency inflation would soon follow.
   II. Interest would still create a rise in the price of goods and services, while diminishing the wages, benefits, and number of employees.

5. **"Due to not being able to charge interest on simple-loan contracts, the government will have no incentive to make the United States Treasury efficient."**

    Why does the government need to charge interest to make a profit when it can create the money it needs in the first place?

6. **"Your currency will be inflationary like the Greenback."**

    There are two reasons as to why the Greenback was inflationary: First, the Exemption Clause in the Legal Tender Act. Second, interest. The author has already discussed the negative effects of interest, thus he will not do so again here. Instead, said author will elaborate on the Exemption Clause.

    According to Sarah Emery in *Seven Financial Conspiracies,* the International Bankers lobbied Congress to incorporate the Exemption Clause into the Legal Tender Act (February 1862). This clause made it where the National Debt, Imports, and Government Bonds had to be paid in gold (which was owned by said International Bankers). As a result, the Federal Government had to print more Greenbacks than were necessary (currency inflation) in order to purchase said gold.

    Basically, it was gold and the bankers that killed the Greenback. Not only that, to add more insult to injury, it was also documented by Sarah Emery that the International Bankers took said Greenbacks to purchase Government Bonds, which resulted in them being compensated with interest. So not only did they get their gold back, but they made a little profit from the government-paid interest as well.

7. **"People need compound interest (401k's or IRA's) to finance their retirements."**

    Under this proposed system, without the risk of losing savings to economic crashes or said savings being made less valuable over time, people can save for retirement without the need of interest. In addition, the reduction in taxation and the price of goods and services will mean people will not need to work a long time or save a lot of money to retire.

8. **"Due to creating its own money, the Federal Government will spend excessively."**

The author will not deny the possibility of this occurring. Thus, it will be the responsibility of the American People (through voting and running for public office) to ensure that such a thing does not happen.

9. **"Lending at interest is not a sin."**
   I. Due to poor scholarship, the word "nokri" in the Deuteronomy 15 and 23 has been translated to the ambiguous term "foreigner." However, according to the linguist James Strong, "nokri" translates to "hostile foreigner" or "enemy." Jesus Christ in Luke 6:35 rescinds this exception. Thus, the Christian is prohibited from charging interest with no exceptions.
   II. The author wants to provide a quote from Jeremiah O'Callaghan:[82]

"The usurers still object that in this text the verb *lend* is not of the imperative, but *optative* mood, importing an evangelical counsel of perfection, merely *recommending* to aim at being the sons of the Most High; but that they, humble souls, aspire to no such dignity, being satisfied to grovel here below in pursuit of the good things of this world: *Wisdom,* ii. 6. I suppose they hold in the same optative mood the other verbs, *love* your enemies, *be merciful; judge not: give,* and it *will* be given you, that are found in the same, and in the following, verses of the gospel. Supposing, for argument sake, that the verb, *lend,* and the others, be taken in the optative sense, what could be the conclusion? Why, but 'that Christ recommends to lend gratis, therefore we will not obey the advice.' Such monstrous impiety, such glaring perversion of the text, is maintained and reduced to practice everyday, by persons calling themselves [Christians] and faithful Ministers of the Gospel."

10. **"Taxation is theft."**
    I. This statement relies upon money being a commodity (a result of interest in moneylending) instead of a tool (which it was originally created to be).
    II. Money is a tool created by the government to ease the exchange of wealth (the fruit of a person's labor and the yield of the land). In other words, it is a public utility that the

---

[82] *Usury or Lending at Interest* (1828), pages 42 to 43.

government maintains through taxation. If the government does not tax the money supply, then currency inflation will occur and the money will become less valuable (which will diminish its effectiveness as public utility).

11. "You're a Communist."

The author has two questions:

I. If Communism is a monopoly conducted by the State, which, in turn, is financed (controlled) by the Capitalists using money they derived from interest, then wouldn't the author (if he is a Communist) be hurting his own cause by fighting against the source of funding for his ideology?[83]

II. If Communism is an oligarchy (a government of non-elected officials), then wouldn't the author (if he is a Communist) be fighting against his ideology by not fighting for the elimination of the United States Constitution, but, instead, fighting for its amending?

12. "Debt Forgiveness is impractical."

Debt forgiveness can be achieved through government decree and enforcement of said decree.[84] In other words, it is not that difficult.

13. "I paid off my debts, so others should pay off theirs."

I. This is not always possible due to situations varying amongst people. For example: Unlike Baby Boomers and Generation X, Millennials, Generation Z, and Generation Alpha are unable to pay off their debts due to inflation, a terrible job market, and low pay.

II. The newly freed money from debt forgiveness will eventually circulate to the people who were debt free prior to said debt forgiveness. For business owners, this will appear in the influx of consumer spending. For workers, this will appear (theoretically)[85] in increased wages and or the creation/increasing of benefits.

---

83 To understand more the author's first question, he recommends Anthony Migchels' article *What is Capitalism?*, which can be located here: https://realcurrencies.wordpress.com/2011/12/20/what-is-capitalism/

84 An example of this is Congress forgiving the debts (PPP Loans) of businesses.

85 The author says "theoretically" because greed on behalf of business owners is still a factor to consider as to why employees don't receive more money.

14. "Give an example of Debt Forgiveness other than the Bible."

Debt Forgiveness was practiced by the nations of Mesopotamia, Greece (Athens), and the Roman Republic.

15. "Give an example of other nations that have implemented a system similar to yours."
   I. The Roman Republic
   II. West Roman Empire (Under the reign of Magnus Maximus)
   III. East Roman Empire (Under the reign of Justinian the Great)
   IV. Germany (Under the reigns of Charlemagne and Adolf Hitler)[86]
   V. England (Under the reigns of Alfred the Great, Edward the Confessor, William the Conqueror, Henry II, Henry III, Edward I, Edward III, Henry VII, and Edward VI)
   VI. France (Under the reign of Louis IX)
   VII. Austria (Town of Worghl – 1932 to 1933)[87]
   VIII. Libya (Under the reign of Muammar Gaddafi)
   IX. Syria[88]
   X. Iran
   XI. Canada (Quebec Colony - 19th Century)[89]
   XII. Massachusetts Bay Colony (Under the Governorship of John Winthrop)[90]

---

86 While Adolf Hitler did have the government of Germany issue its own debt-free currency, he did not outlaw interest in moneylending.

87 *Interest and Inflation Free Money* by Margrit Kennedy, pages 14 and 15

88 https://www.activistpost.com/2012/09/state-owned-central-banks-are-real.html

89 *Usury, or Lending at Interest* (1828) by Jeremiah O'Callaghan, page 13.

90 *Usury in Christendom: The Mortal Sin that Was and Now is Not* by Michael Hoffman II, pages 225 to 241.

Appendix: "Economy of the Promised Land"
by Anthony Migchels

One reason why we have a few money lenders and landlords running the whole world, with the rest of us toiling as serfs to pay their monthly dues to them, is because we have no real inkling of how we would live without them.

And the difference is so enormous, that one shies away from speaking of it, for fear of being condemned as a foolish Utopian.

But here are a few characteristics of a Usury-free society with a liberated Commons and current technological levels:

- A man would work a maximum of 15 weeks per year to provide for his wife and children.
- Self-Employment and Small Business would be the norm. Wages would be for the young and the simple.
- Men and women would see stress levels decline dramatically. They would spend far more time with each other, their children, their families, and their friends.
- By far most people would live a very comfortable middle class existence. There would still be a few rich people, but they would be much less rich and not able to dominate society because of their wealth.
- Building would see costs decline by 80 to 90%. An architectural revival and boom of uncanny proportions can be expected.
- Every man and his family would have access to decent land and living and working space at very low cost. By far most people would own some land, but vast landholdings would no longer exist because there would be no renting.
- Food production would be heavily decentralized and many families would grow at least some food themselves. Food quality would improve incredibly.
- Poverty would be out of the question. There would still be differences in class, but they would be more about genetics and education and not about wealth. But there would be no disenfranchised underclass and only the most problematic people would be unable to join the

general well being. The barbarization of the poor would end and a great emancipation of those now oppressed by Usury and wage-slavery will result.

- There would be no Big Pharma (owned by the Banks) to war on Natural Health. Combined with low stress and excellent nutrition, health (both physical and psychological) and longevity would grow substantially. Substance abuse would decline.

- There would be no Trillions for the Plutocrats to fund all these problems aimed at distracting us and centralizing power. No Migration, no Climate Change, no Bankers orchestrating many and enormous wars. There would be no funding for endless fake news, bogus "science," or devious ideologies aimed at dividing people.

- Families and local communities will have plenty of funding for their own needs.

- General corruption levels would decline immensely.

- Urbanization would decline and the countryside would be repopulated, as abundant money would revive local economies, and there would be no Plutocratic landholdings keeping people out.

- There would still be inequality, but based on merit and added value, not on property. Hard work and achievement would be rewarded. Wealth inequality levels would be far lower, though. What is more, money will no longer be the main driver of status. Aristocracy will be based on service. On spiritual and intellectual excellence, not on the acquisition of treasure.

- The State would decline very seriously in scope and impact, returning to its basic jobs of providing a basic legal system and defense, not endless nannying and other massive overreaches. Although this remains an important issue in itself. National Socialism, for instance, created a massive totalitarian State supposedly to "fight unearned income" and "provide for the citizenry." But the real aim and focus of economic decentralization is to promote autonomy and economic independence for the common man. This is the core issue. When this goal is achieved, nobody will need a big State to depend on.

- And there is of course Lietaer's question: "What would the Cathedrals of the 21st Century look like?" With interest-free lending, major, very long-term investments become viable again. It took European cities a century to build a cathedral, back in the days of the Usury-free Catholic economy. What would people build today, if they had a hundred years to create it?

This is what is at stake and this is what they have stolen from us. This is how we would live, without Usury, without the landowners, without the speculations. Without the parasites who add nothing and have everything. Without their silly "making money with money" schemes, which have no other purpose than exploiting the toil of the masses – a.k.a. Capitalism.

Note that for all this no ideology is needed. Just the acceptance of reality that money does not grow automatically in a bank account and that only labor creates wealth.

That we all need a fair deal.

A man produces easily enough for at least five people to live well. This is the reality. We have the duty to ourselves to claim this production for ourselves and our loved ones.

To say "No" to Slavery and "Yes" to what basically amounts to the Promise Land.

A Review by Metin Ozsavran

A Critically Important Proposal to Save America!

September 10, 2017

It's an honest direct, purposeful writing by a humble Black American writer who is trying to help his country despite all the hardships given to blacks in the past. It's not long winded and philosophical. Its useful as a tool like a sharp knife cutting through all the fake media clutter to bring relief to real hard working American People.

Capitalism is not a sacred religion, nor is it from God himself. Capitalism is not America. America is Free Enterprise. They are not one and the same thing. Quite the opposite nowadays. Capitalism is not giving people opportunity, it's hurting and squeezing them now. Capitalism has outlived its useful lifetime. To be "Great Again," America needs to solve, understand, embrace and develop a post-capitalistic world. This critical little volume must be examined by the current President's team very carefully, and developed upon, if he really wants to "Make America Great Again."

The world does not need a weak, corrupted, poisoned, rabid dog America, attacking everywhere to get some scraps. We need a healthy, productive, creative America, leading the world with goodness, not threats. Each constitution, each law has a lifetime until the crooks develop ways to circumvent it. As they do, we need new laws to reign them in again. That's why like everything else, the current American constitution must be re-sharpened. Mr. Pope-Williams has poured his heart and resources to contribute something to his nation, instead of preying on it like everyone else. This book must be picked up by major publishers and discussed over in most serious forums in America.

Regular Americans will do much good to their country by buying this book in quantity for Christmas and giving copies to friends.

Bibliography

- http://ebible.org/web/
- *History of Money and Usury in America* by Daniel Krynicki
- http://watson.brown.edu/costsofwar/costs/economic
- *Digest of the Divine Law* by Howard Rand.
- https://realcurrencies.wordpress.com/2012/01/05/debt-free-money-alone-does-not-solve-compound-interest/
- *Usury in Christendom: The Mortal Sin that Was and Now is Not* by Michael Hoffman II.
- http://en.wikipedia.org/wiki/Fungible
- http://www.taxpolicycenter.org/briefing-book/how-much-does-federal-government-spend-health-care
- https://ed.gov/about/overview/budget/index.html?src=rt
- https://www.themarshallproject.org/2015/02/12/the-cost-of-crime-fighting#.oLf0aUObO
- http://www.usgovernmentspending.com/us_welfare_spending_40.html
- *Secrets of the Federal Reserve* by Eustace Mullins.
- http://www.economiccures.com/
- http://www.sourcenewspapers.com/opinion/guest-column-bill-would-end-corporate-secrecy-to-fight-terrorism/article_fd524d1c-d93e-582d-b47a-ba9aa2c80dc2.html
- https://www.linkedin.com/pulse/organic-economy-vs-fake-paper-metin-ozsavran?trk=mp-reader-card
- http://www.ohchr.org/EN/ProfessionalInterest/Pages/CESCR.aspx
- www.dictionary.com
- http://www.usccb.org/about/pro-life-activities/respect-life-program/2014/poverty-and-abortion.cfm
- *Usury or Lending at Interest* (1828) by Jeremiah O'Callaghan

www.ingramcontent.com/pod-product-compliance
Lightning Source LLC
Chambersburg PA
CBHW081155180526
45170CB00006B/2089